Letts
gets you through

KS2 MATHS
SATs SUCCESS
REVISION GUIDE

Ages 7–11

KS2
MATHS
SATs

REVISION
GUIDE

SHAUN STIRLING

Numbers

Calculations

Fractions, Decimals, Percentages

Ratio and Proportion

Place value

Numbers are made up of **digits**. The position of each digit in a number shows what it stands for. This is known as **place value**. Whole numbers are called **integers**.

Look at the digit **five** in these whole numbers below. Its value changes depending on its place in the number.

Number in digits	Number in words	Value of five digit
5	**five**	5
54	**fifty**-four	50
523	**five** hundred and twenty-three	500
5178	**five** thousand, one hundred and seventy-eight	5000
50 411	**fifty** thousand, four hundred and eleven	50 000
539 902	**five** hundred and thirty-nine thousand, nine hundred and two	500 000

Can you see how each time the digit moves one place to the left, it becomes ten times as big? What happens when it moves one place to the right?

Example question: Lauren and Grace are playing a video game.

Lauren's score = **66 780**   Grace's score = **66 695**
Who has the highest score?

The ten thousands and the thousands digits are both the same, but if you move one more place to the right you can see that Lauren has a 7 in the hundreds place but Grace only has a 6. So, Lauren has the highest score.

Roman Numerals

Roman numerals are a number system used by the Romans that is still used today. You might see digits on a clock or dates written in Roman numerals.

I	V	X	L	C	D	M
1	**5**	**10**	**50**	**100**	**500**	**1000**

Putting a letter after or before a larger one means you add or subtract that amount from this number. So Henry VIII is Henry the 8th because 5 is followed by three 1s but George IV is George the 4th because 5 has a 1 written before it.

Example question: Here is a date written in Roman numerals. **MMIX**
Write the number in figures.
The two Ms represent 2000. I before X is 1 less than 10, which is 9.
2000 add 9 is 2009.

Listen up
1

Comparing numbers

When comparing numbers, you can use **symbols** to show which is the smaller and which is the larger number:

- > is greater than
- < is smaller than

Example question: Insert either **=**, **<** or **>** between these pairs of operations.

12 × 10	240 ÷ 2
75 + 45	200 − 60
0.25 + 0.5	0.6 + 0.1

Work out each operation and then choose the correct symbol.

120	=	120
120	<	140
0.75	>	0.7

Top tip!

When using the smaller than and greater than symbols (< and >), it is helpful to think of a crocodile's mouth opening to eat the larger number. For example:

24 345 < 25 358

Keywords

Digit ➤ Individual figures that make up numbers

Place value ➤ The place of each digit shows its value in the number

Integer ➤ Whole numbers, which can be positive or negative – they cannot be fractions or decimal numbers

Roman numerals ➤ A number system using seven letters to represent number values.

Have a go!

With a partner, take turns to roll four dice. Rearrange the dice to make a four-digit number. The winner is the person who makes the number closest to 3000.

Test yourself

1. Arrange these numbers in order, smallest first.
   12 121, 12 221, 10 221, 11 222, 12 112, 10 212

2. What is the largest odd number you can make from these digits? 4 7 3 8 1 5

3. Put either < or > between these four numbers to make the sequence correct.
   303   103   301   130

4. Write the year MCMLXX in digits.

5. Write the number four million, eight hundred and three thousand, six hundred and two in digits.

Rounding numbers

You can use **rounding** when you don't have to be accurate with your answer. This makes big numbers easier to work with and gives an approximate answer to an operation before using a written method.

You might have to round to the nearest **ten**, **hundred** or **thousand**.

For decimal numbers it might be useful to round to the nearest **integer** (whole number).

Example question: 135 725 people attended a music festival. Round the attendance to the nearest thousand, hundred and ten.

	Nearest 1000	Nearest 100	Nearest 10
Actual attendance	135 725	135 725	135 725
	Look at the hundreds digit, 7. Because it is 5 or more, round up the thousands to 6000.	Look at the tens digit, 2. Because it is less than five, the hundreds stay as 700.	Look at the ones digit, 5. Because it is 5 or more, round up the tens to 30.
	136 000	135 700	135 730

2

Rounding money to the nearest pound or ten pence is useful when you are shopping for a few items. You might want to round up to make sure you have enough cash when it's time to pay!

Negative numbers

Numbers are either positive or negative. A negative number has a minus sign before it.

Negative numbers are used in algebra and graphs with four quadrants. Temperatures can have negative numbers.

Example question: At the Antarctic Research Station the outside temperature is –39°C. Inside it is 18°C. What is the difference in temperature?

When solving problems like this it is helpful to draw a number line. You can then jump from the negative outdoor temperature to the positive indoor temperature to find the difference.

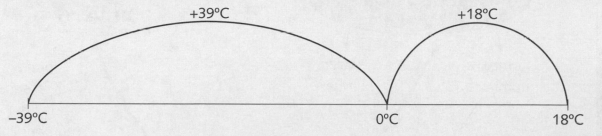

Add the two jumps together, crossing the zero to find the total temperature difference. 39°C + 18°C = **57°C** warmer inside the station.

Keywords

Rounding ➤ Changing a big number to one that's easier to work with, for example the nearest ten, hundred or thousand

Negative numbers ➤ Numbers less than zero

Have a go! Ask an adult to show you a car odometer. This measures how far the car has travelled. Round the total mileage to the nearest ten, hundred and thousand miles.

Test yourself

1. 74 738 fans attended the Football World Cup Final. Round this number to the nearest ten, hundred and thousand.

2. During the day the temperature was 6°C. Overnight it dropped by 14°C. What was the overnight temperature?

Numbers

This mind map will help you remember all the main points from this topic. Have a go at drawing your own mind map.

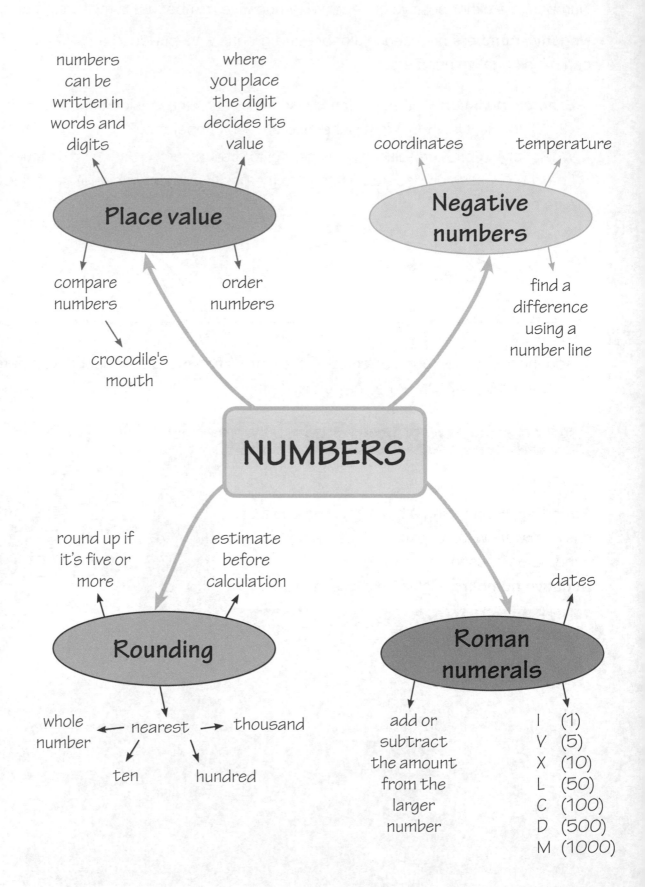

numbers can be written in words and digits

where you place the digit decides its value

coordinates

temperature

Place value

Negative numbers

compare numbers

order numbers

find a difference using a number line

crocodile's mouth

NUMBERS

round up if it's five or more

estimate before calculation

dates

Rounding

Roman numerals

whole number ← nearest → thousand

add or subtract the amount from the larger number

I	(1)
V	(5)
X	(10)
L	(50)
C	(100)
D	(500)
M	(1000)

ten   hundred

1 Write this number in digits. **(1 mark)**
Three million, sixty-three thousand, nine hundred and two.

....

2 Write this number in words: 1 207 708 .... **(1 mark)**

....

3 Use the digits 2, 3, 7, 8 and 1 to make the following:

a. the largest odd number .... **(1 mark)**

b. the smallest odd number .... **(1 mark)**

c. the largest even number .... **(1 mark)**

d. the smallest even number .... **(1 mark)**

4 Complete this series of Roman numerals. **(2 marks)**

LXVI, LXVII, ..., ..., LXX, ..., ...

5 **a.** Multiply 34 908 by 10 .... **(1 mark)**

b. Divide 65 000 by 10 .... **(1 mark)**

6 Put < or > between the numbers to make the number sentences correct.
(2 marks)

a. 212 313 ☐ 213 231 **b.** 5 542 134 ☐ 5 543 135

7 In July 747 936 people visited the British Museum. How many is this, when rounded to the nearest: **(3 marks)**

a. ten? .... **b.** hundred? ....

c. thousand? ....

8 How many different whole numbers are there that make 50 when rounded to the nearest 10? Is this the same for every multiple of 10? **(1 mark)**

....

9 What is £3.56 rounded to the nearest pound? .... **(1 mark)**

10 In New York the temperature during the day was 13°C. Overnight it dropped to −7°C. How much lower was this? **(1 mark)**

....

BIDMAS

When you have a number sentence that has more than one **operation**, you need to know which order to do them in.

For example, what is the answer to 6 + 5 × 3?
Is it 21 or 33?

Luckily there is a set of rules that make it clear and provide a handy way to remember them:

Brackets

Indices

Division

Multiplication

Addition

Subtraction

Brackets: make sure that you complete any operations that are inside brackets **first**.

Indices: this means powers such as **squares** or **cubes**. Do these next.

Division and Multiplication: work from left to right to solve these operations. They are equally important.

Addition and Subtraction: like division and multiplication they are equally important. Tackle these **last**, working from left to right.

So the answer to 6 + 5 × 3 is 21 because multiplication must be done before addition.

Example question: Write the correct sign **<**, **>** or **=** in the following number sentence.

3 × (10 + 3) ☐ (3 × 10) − 5

3 × 13 ☐ 30 − 5 ◄─────

> **First** work out each side of the number sentence. Follow BIDMAS! Remove the brackets.

39 ☐ 25 ◄─────

> Then complete the operations. You can now see which side is greater so put in the correct symbol.

39 > 25

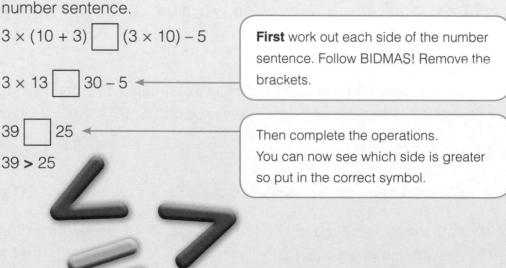

Keywords

Operation ➤ Grown-ups will know these as sums. They could be adding, subtracting, multiplying or dividing. Operations might also be things like squaring a number

Square ➤ To find the square of a whole number, you multiply it by itself. You will already know a few square numbers through the times tables, for example $4 \times 4 = 16$. You can show that a number is squared with a symbol, for example $9^2 = 81$

Cube ➤ To find the cube of a number, you multiply it by itself twice. For example, 4 cubed is 64 because $4 \times 4 \times 4 = 64$. You can show that a number is cubed with a symbol, for example $5^3 = 125$

Listen up **3**

Although you might be used to using an electronic calculator, for example to find the cube of a large number, students are not permitted to use one in any part of the maths tests.

Parent tip!

Have a go!

Make ten cards with these digits and symbols.

See how many different totals you can make using all four digit cards, two operations and brackets.

Test yourself

1. $120 - 20 \times 3 = ?$
2. $60 - 75 \div 15 = ?$
3. Place the right symbol <, > or = between these number sentences.

   $(6^2 - 4) + 8 \;\square\; 2 \times (4^2 + 4)$
4. What two numbers could go in the spaces to make this correct?

   $(\square - \square) \times 9 = 45$

Multiples

When you multiply two **integers** you create a **multiple** of both numbers. Learn your times tables and you will know multiples of all integers up to 12 × 12. There are **rules of divisibility** that will help you to spot multiples of many numbers.

Multiple of	Rule of divisibility
2	An even number. The last digit is 0, 2, 4, 6 or 8
3	The **digital sum** is a multiple of 3
4	Even number **and** the last two digits are a multiple of 4
5	The last digit is either 0 or 5
6	Even number with a digital sum that is a multiple of 3
8	When you halve it, it is a multiple of 4 (see above)
9	The digital sum is 9
10	The last digit is 0
50	The last digits are 50 or 00
100	The last digits are 00

Factors

It is useful to know the **factors** of whole numbers when working with fractions and algebra. If you know your times tables, you will know the factors of many numbers.

For example the factors of 24 are 1, 2, 3, 4, 6, 8, 12 and 24 because…

$1 \times 24 = 24$
$2 \times 12 = 24$
$3 \times 8 = 24$
$4 \times 6 = 24$

Most numbers have an even number of factors. **Prime numbers** have only two, and square numbers (e.g. 9) have an odd number of factors. Can you think why?

Top tip!

Think of numbers in multiple families. The 3s, 6s and 9s all have digital sums of 3 while the 2s, 4s and 8s are all even.

Listen up
4

Common factors

If two different whole numbers share some of the same factors, these are called their common factors. It's easier to see this on a Venn diagram.

From the Venn diagram you can see that the **common factors** of 24 and 15 are 1 and 3. The **highest common factor** is 3.

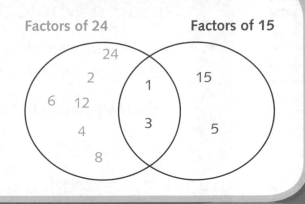

Keywords

Multiple ➤ If a number divides by another without leaving a remainder, then it's a multiple of that number. For example 48 is a multiple of both 6 and 8 because $48 \div 6 = 8$

Digital sum ➤ Find the digital sum of a number by adding the digits together until you get to a single digit number. For example the digital sum of 909 is 9 so you know that it is a multiple of 9 ($9 + 0 + 9 = 18$, $1 + 8 = 9$)

Factor ➤ A whole number that divides exactly into another whole number. For example both 6 and 8 are factors of 48 because they divide into 48 without leaving a remainder

Prime number ➤ A whole number that has exactly two factors, one and itself. For example 7 has factors 1 and 7. 1 isn't a prime number because it only has one factor!

Work with a partner.
You will need number cards from 0 – 50. Draw a Venn diagram.

Secretly decide upon rules for each 'hoop', e.g. factors of 7 and 6.

Your partner's task is to figure out the rules.

Start placing cards onto the diagram in the right zones.

How many cards can you place before your partner works out your rules?

Swap roles.

❶ Circle the multiples of nine.
2081, 6372, 4173, 1332

❷ Circle the multiples of eight.
520, 1788, 6296, 256

❸ Write a three-digit number that is a multiple of five and nine.

❹ List the prime numbers between 40 and 50.

❺ What are the missing numbers?

An even number with nine as a factor will also have __ and __ as factors.

Adding whole numbers

Here is a written method for **adding** two or more numbers together including decimals. This is the **standard column method**.

Example question: What is the total of 6924 + 758?

```
    7 5 8
 + 6 9 2 4
         2
       1
```

Write both numbers with digits lined up in columns. Add the digits in the ones column, 8 + 4 = 12. Make a note of the 10 from 12 in the tens column. The 2 stays in the ones.

```
    7 5 8
 + 6 9 2 4
   7 6 8 2
   1   1
```

Add the digits in the tens column, 5 + 2 + 1 = 8. Repeat with all the remaining columns. If you make a hundred or a thousand, make a note of it **below** the line and include it when adding the column.

Adding decimals

You can use the same column method to add **decimals**. Make sure you line up the decimal points before adding each column. This is especially important when the numbers have different numbers of digits.

It's a good idea to make an **estimate** first. You can check your answer against this at the end to make sure it's about right.

Example question: What is the sum of 4.56 and 24.8?

Before you start estimate the answer using **rounding**.
4.56 and 24.8 are 5 and 25 when rounded to the nearest whole number. 5 + 25 = 30 so your answer should be close to 30.

```
    4.5 6
 + 2 4.8
     .3 6
       1
```

Write the numbers in columns. Line up the **decimal point**. Start at the right by adding the hundredths, 6 + 0. Next add the tenths, 0.5 + 0.8 = 1.3. Make a note of the 1 from 1.3 in the ones column while the 3 stays in the tenths column.

```
    4.5 6
 + 2 4.8
   2 9.3 6
       1
```

Add up all the remaining columns. Check your answer against your **estimate**. 29.36 is pretty close to 30!

Solving problems

You will need to use the **addition method** to solve problems. These problems might have one or several steps.

Top tip! When adding up columns, look for pairs of numbers that make ten, or for doubles, and add them first.

Example question:
Jamil attends a drama club throughout the year.

If Jamil pays in advance for the whole year he will get a discount.

It will cost him £220. If he does this, how much will he save?

Special offers!

	Fees
Autumn	£92.70
Spring	£72.10
Summer	£82.40
Whole year special offer – discount	£220.00

First add the fees for the three terms. Use the column method.

```
   £ 9 2.7 0
+  £ 7 2.1 0
   £ 8 2.4 0
   ─────────
   £ 2 4 7.2 0
     2   1
```

Then compare this total to the discounted price. You shouldn't need a column method for this. £247.20 – £220 = £27.20

So, Jamil would save **£27.20**

Keywords

Adding ➤ Calculating the total or sum of numbers
Estimating ➤ Making a rough or approximate calculation
Decimal point ➤ A dot used to separate the decimal fraction from the whole part of a number

Listen up 5

Have a go! Collect all the receipts for your family's food shopping for a week. Use the column addition method to find how much was spent.

Test yourself

❶ Calculate:

a. 3725 + 487 =

b. 635 + 7673 =

c. 495 + 45 + 802 =

❷ Lee needs a new football kit. The shirt costs £24.95, the shorts £17.99 and the socks £5.49. How much change will he get from £50?

Number lines

You will need a written method for **subtracting** one larger number from another. You could use a number line to do this – you may have used number lines to count up from a smaller to a larger number.

Example question: Calculate 702 – 687

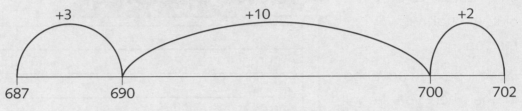

Add the 'jumps' together to find the difference between the two numbers. 3 + 10 + 2 = **15** so 702 – 687 = 15

This method is especially good if the numbers you are subtracting are close together.

Column method

Example question: What is 634 minus 357?

$$6 \ ^2\!3 \ ^1\!4$$
$$- \ 3 \ 5 \ 7$$
$$\overline{ \ 7}$$

Write both numbers clearly with the digits lined up. Begin with the ones column. Although 634 is a bigger number, the ones digit (4) is smaller. Exchange a ten for ten ones. 14 – 7 = 7.

$$^5\!6 \ ^{12}\!3 \ ^1\!4$$
$$- \ 3 \ 5 \ 7$$
$$\overline{ \ 7 \ 7}$$

Next tackle the tens column. Once again the digit is smaller. Exchange a hundred for ten tens. 12 – 5 = 7.

$$^5\!6 \ ^{12}\!3 \ ^1\!4$$
$$- \ 3 \ 5 \ 7$$
$$\overline{2 \ 7 \ 7}$$

Finally deal with the hundreds column.
500 – 300 = 200.

Addition is the **inverse** of subtraction, so you can use it to check your answer. In this example 357 + 277 = 634.

Problems

You will need to use your subtraction method to solve problems.
These might have one or several steps.

Example question: Ruby and Sam travel for their summer holiday.
Ruby drives 143 km before flying 3447 km. Sam flies 1368 km before
driving another 624 km. How much further does Ruby travel than Sam?

> First find the totals for Ruby's and Sam's journeys.

143 km + 3447 km = 3590 km   624 km + 1368 km = 1992 km

> Then subtract Sam's total from Ruby's total to find the difference.

3590 km − 1992 km = **1598 km**

> Remember to use the units of measurement in your answer.

Parent tip! Talk to your child about the written methods they use in school. Perhaps the school has a calculations strategy that all classes use.

Keywords

Subtracting ➤ Taking one number away from another to find the difference between them. Other words for subtraction are take away or minus

Inverse ➤ The inverse or opposite operation can be used to check your answer, e.g. use addition to check a subtraction answer; use multiplication to check a division answer

Have a go! From a pack of cards, remove all the picture cards and the tens. Deal four cards to each player. From the remaining deck, turn up two cards to make a 2-digit target number. Each player then uses their cards to make two 2-digit numbers so that when they are subtracted, they are as close as possible to the target number.

Test yourself

1 Calculate:
   a. 1145 − 871 =   c. 27.4 − 19.3 =
   b. 4221 − 2987 =   d. 99 − 0.76 =

2 Roshan and Sara both buy a magazine. Roshan pays with a £5 note and receives £1.50 change. Sara pays with a £10 note and receives £7.15 change. How much more does Roshan's magazine cost than Sara's?

The grid method

Adults might not have learned the grid method at school. This **informal method** can help you understand how to **partition** and **multiply** bigger numbers.

Example question: Work out 25 × 347

First, partition both numbers into hundreds, tens and ones. Write these values alongside the spaces in your grid.

Next multiply the pairs of numbers, filling the answers into the spaces in the grid.

Now add up each row and finish by using your column addition method to find the total.

	300	40	7		
20	6000	800	140	=	6 9 4 0
5	1500	200	35	=	+ 1 7 3 5

$$6940 + 1735 = 8675$$

So, 25 × 347 = **8675**

Short and long multiplication

Just as with the other three operations, you may need to use a **formal written method** to multiply large numbers. These are tried and tested methods that grown-ups will be familiar with.

Example question: What is 482 × 6?

Before starting, make an **estimate**. This is close to 500 × 6 so the answer should be about 3000.

```
  4 8 2
×     6
      2
    1
```

Set out your numbers carefully in columns for this **short multiplication**. Begin on the right with the ones, 6 × 2 = 12. Make a note of the ten from 12 in the tens column while the 2 stays in the ones.

```
  4 8 2
×     6
2 8 9 2
  4 1
```

Next, multiply the tens by 6. Add that extra ten to the total. 6 × 8 + 1 = 49. The four tens go below the line.

Then, multiply the hundreds by 6. Add the four tens.

6 × 4 + 4 = 28. Your answer includes a thousand so put this in a new column.

So, 482 × 6 = **2892**

The answer is close to the estimate of 3000.

Listen up 7

Short and long multiplication (continued)

With bigger numbers it will take longer using **long multiplication**.

Example question: What is 143 × 27?

$$\begin{array}{r} {}^{3}1\,{}^{2}4\,3 \\ \times\quad 2\,7 \\ \hline 1\,0\,0\,1 \end{array}$$

You will need to partition 27 into 20 + 7 and do two sets of multiplication. Start with 7 × 143. Use the same method as short multiplication. Carry any tens, hundreds or thousands you make into the next column. Make a note of them above each number.

$$\begin{array}{r} {}^{3}1\,{}^{2}4\,3 \\ \times\quad 2\,7 \\ \hline 1\,0\,0\,1 \\ 2\,8\,6\,0 \end{array}$$

Next multiply 20 × 143. Because you are multiplying by a multiple of ten (20) place a zero in the ones column before you start. Ignore the numbers you carried last time.

$$\begin{array}{r} {}^{3}1\,{}^{2}4\,3 \\ \times\quad 2\,7 \\ \hline 1\,0\,0\,1 \\ 2\,8\,6\,0 \\ \hline 3\,8\,6\,1 \end{array}$$

Finally use the column addition method to add the two multiplications.

So, 143 × 27 = **3861**

Top tip! When multiplying multiples of ten or a hundred, the number of zeros in your answer will be the same as in the two numbers you are multiplying, e.g. 40 × 6**00** = 24**000**.

Keywords

Multiplying ➤ A short way to add the same number together many times, also called 'lots of'. You will need to know the multiplication tables

Partition ➤ Breaking up a number into its separate parts, e.g. hundreds, tens and ones, to help you complete operations like multiplication

Have a go! To use any of these methods you must know the times tables. Ask someone to test you and make a list of a few tricky ones that you get wrong. Can you find ways to remember them? For example 56 = 7 × 8 (the digits come in order).

Test yourself

❶ Calculate:
   a. 7614 × 23 =
   b. 67 × 35 =
   c. 292 × 89 =

❷ Amar saves 75p a week. How much has he saved after 15 weeks?

Calculations

Division can seem the trickiest of the four operations. Remember that it's the **inverse** of **multiplication**, and you use the times tables to help you.

Repeated subtraction

Like the grid for multiplication, this method (also known as 'chunking') is one that grown-ups might not know. You subtract multiples of the **divisor** from your starting number.

Example question: Work out $622 \div 28$

Start with an estimate. This is close to $600 \div 30$ so the answer should be about 20.

```
   ⁵⁶1²2 2
 –  2 8 0   (10 × 28)
   ²³1⁴4 2
 –  2 8 0   (10 × 28)
      6 2
```

Subtract multiples of 28 from 622 until you have nothing or a remainder.

Start by taking away ten lots of 28. Remember your column subtraction method here. $622 - 280 = 342$
Next subtract another ten lots of 28. $342 - 280 = 62$

```
   ⁵⁶ 1²2 2
 –  2 8 0   (10 × 28)
   ²³1 ⁴4 2
 –  2 8 0   (10 × 28)
      ⁵⁶ 1²2
 –    5 6   (2 × 28)
         6
```

You have 62 left. Take two lots of 28.
You are left with a **remainder** of 6.
If you add up all the multiples (or chunks) that you have taken away, that is the answer.
$10 + 10 + 2 = 22$ with a remainder of 6.

$622 \div 28 =$ **22r6**. That's close to the estimate of 20.

Keywords

Division ➤ The **inverse** of multiplication
Divisor ➤ The amount that you are dividing by – it might be a whole number, a fraction or a decimal
Remainder ➤ What's left over when the number you are dividing is not a multiple of the divisor (can be an integer, fraction or decimal). In problems you usually have to round your remainder either up or down

Top tip!

Division is the inverse of multiplication. So every multiplication fact is also a division. For example:
$6 \times 7 = 42$ or $42 \div 7 = 6$
Learn one get one free!

Listen up 8

Short and long division

Grown-ups will be more familiar with these formal written methods.

Example question: Work out 278 ÷ 5

$$5\overline{)27^28}\quad =\quad 55r3$$

In this **short division**, take the first two digits (27) of the number and divide them by five. 27 ÷ 5 = 5 remainder 2. Carry the remainder into the next column. This makes a new two digit number: 28.

28 ÷ 5 = 5 remainder 3

So, 278 ÷ 5 = **55r3**

You can write your remainder as a fraction. Because you are dividing by five, the remainder is $\frac{3}{5}$. So 278 ÷ 5 = **$55\frac{3}{5}$**

Long division will help you to write any remainder as a **decimal**. Subtract as you did for repeated subtraction but 'draw down' digits from above.

Example question: 476 rugby fans go to see a game. Each coach carries 56 fans. How many coaches will they need?

$$56\overline{)476.}\quad=8.5$$
$$\underline{448}$$
$$280$$

Set your numbers out like you did for short division.

56 won't go into 47 so don't put anything in the tens column. Eight lots of 56 are 448, record this and subtract from 476. Put an eight in the hundreds column.

You have a remainder of 28. You could stop here with your answer being 8r28. Add a decimal point and bring down a zero from above to find the remainder as a decimal.

280 ÷ 56 = 5 so your final right answer is 8.5 or $8\frac{1}{2}$.

You can't have half a coach! Eight coaches won't be enough so round up to **nine** coaches.

Whichever written method you use, you will have to decide to either **round up** or **round down** your remainder.

Have a go! Explain the methods you use for all four operations to a grown-up. Are the operations like the methods they used when they were at school?

Test yourself

❶ Calculate:

a. 854 ÷ 7 =   b. 348 ÷ 12 =

c. £364 ÷ 8 =

❷ Aisling has 990 ml of cola. How many 150 ml glasses can she fill?

Calculations

This mind map will help you remember all the main points from this topic. Have a go at drawing your own mind map.

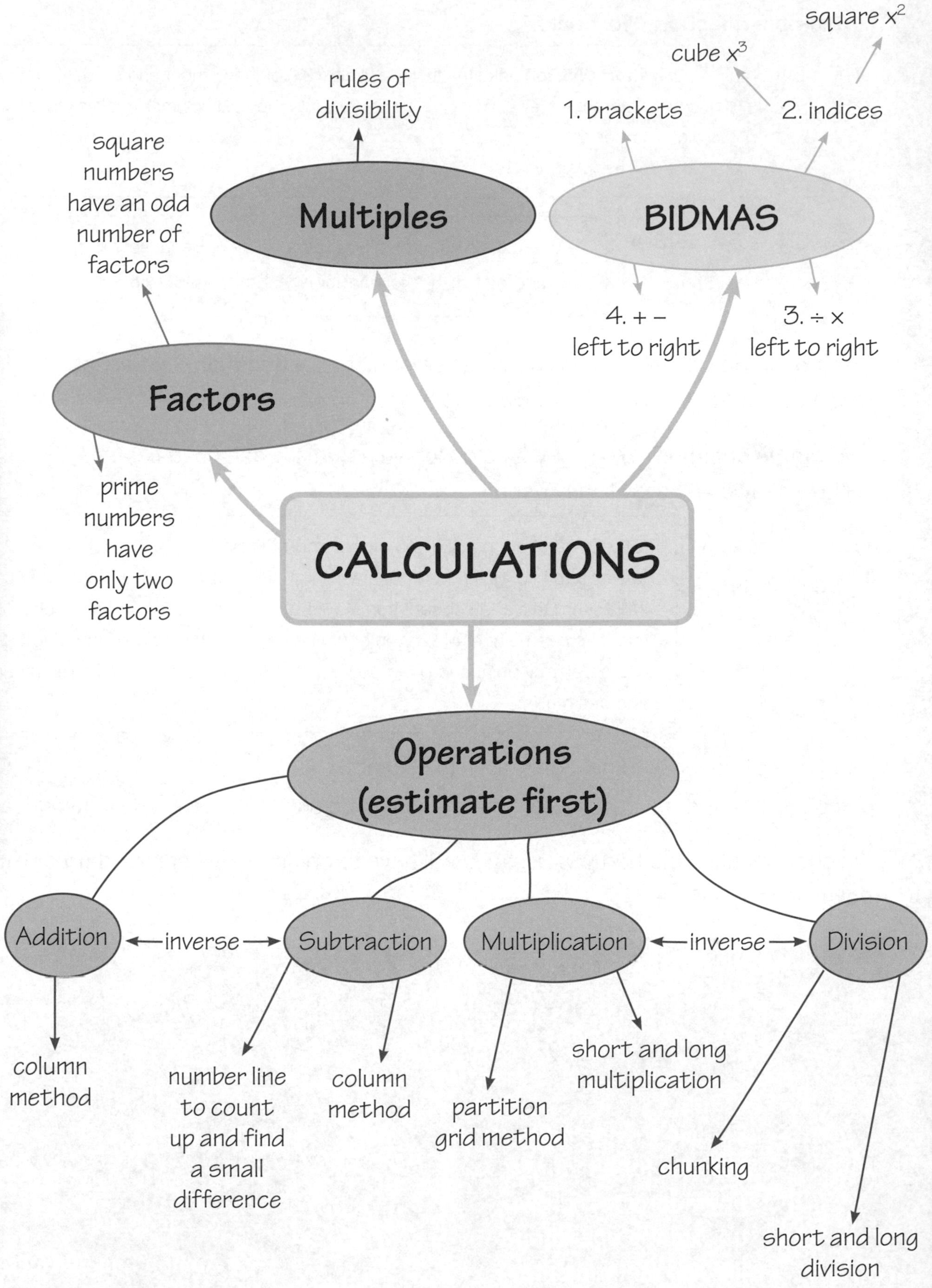

rules of divisibility

square x^2

cube x^3

1. brackets

2. indices

square numbers have an odd number of factors

Multiples

BIDMAS

4. + −
left to right

3. ÷ ×
left to right

Factors

prime numbers have only two factors

CALCULATIONS

Operations (estimate first)

Addition ← inverse → Subtraction

Multiplication ← inverse → Division

column method

number line to count up and find a small difference

column method

partition grid method

short and long multiplication

chunking

short and long division

1 Write the correct symbol: **<, >** or **=**.

   a. $(3 \times 6) + 2$ ☐ $48 - 4^2$ **(1 mark)**

   b. $33 - 2 \times 9$ ☐ $100 \div 4 - 10$ **(1 mark)**

2 What two numbers could make this number sentence correct?   **(1 mark)**

   $20 - ($ ☐ $\times$ ☐ $) = 5^2 - 23$

3 Are these true or false? (✓ or ✗)

   a. All multiples of 5 are also multiples of 10. ☐   **(1 mark)**

   b. All multiples of 6 are also multiples of 3. ☐   **(1 mark)**

   c. Multiples of 7 end in a 1, 4 or 8. ☐   **(1 mark)**

   d. 609 is a multiple of 9. ☐   **(1 mark)**

4 What are the common factors of 18 and 12?   **(1 mark)**

....

5 What is the largest two-digit prime number? ☐   **(1 mark)**

6 Calculato:

   a. $127.4 + 56.87 =$ ....   **(1 mark)**

   b. $2067 - 189 =$ ....   **(1 mark)**

   c. $56 \times 34 =$ ....   **(1 mark)**

   d. $7248 \div 6 =$ ....   **(1 mark)**

7 Julia has £300. She buys a tablet computer for £258.95 and a
case for £24.95. How much money does she have left?   **(1 mark)**

....

8 Chen is planning a party for 58 guests. Cakes come in packs of four.

   a. How many packs will he need to buy?   **(1 mark)**

....

   b. Each pack of cakes costs £1.25. How much will he need to spend?

                                                             (1 mark)

....

Fractions

There are usually two ways of working with **fractions**.

- To represent numbers that are not **integers**. For example, $5\frac{3}{4}$ is more than 5 but less than 6.
- To find fractions of shapes or quantities. For example, you might have to find a **quarter** of a rectangle or **four-fifths** of £25.00.

Fractions, together with **decimals** and **percentages**, are all used to show parts of a whole. You will need to be able to change between all three.

For example $\frac{1}{4} = 0.25 = 25\%$

Equivalent fractions

Equivalent fractions look different but have the same value.

For example, you might eat half a pizza while your friend eats two-quarters. You have both eaten the same amount. $\frac{1}{2} = \frac{2}{4}$

In a fraction:
- the top number is the **numerator**
- the bottom number is the **denominator**

$\frac{3}{4}$ ← numerator / denominator

To find equivalent fractions, you must either **multiply** or **divide** the numerator and denominator by the same amount.

Example question: Complete the missing number in the box.

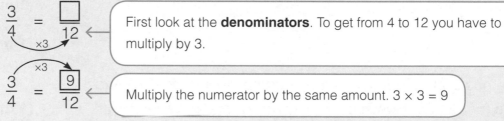

$\frac{3}{4} = \frac{\Box}{12}$ (×3) — First look at the **denominators**. To get from 4 to 12 you have to multiply by 3.

$\frac{3}{4} = \frac{9}{12}$ (×3) — Multiply the numerator by the same amount. $3 \times 3 = 9$

You might have to **reduce** or simplify a fraction to get the smallest possible numerator and denominator. Use **factors** to do this.

Example question: Reduce $\frac{24}{32}$ to its **simplest** terms.

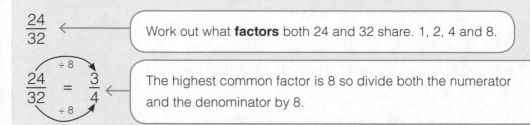

$\frac{24}{32}$ ← Work out what **factors** both 24 and 32 share. 1, 2, 4 and 8.

$\frac{24}{32} = \frac{3}{4}$ (÷8) — The highest common factor is 8 so divide both the numerator and the denominator by 8.

Improper fractions

In **improper fractions** the **numerator** is bigger than the **denominator**.

To change improper fractions to **mixed numbers**, divide the numerator by the denominator. Your answer will be a whole number with any remainder added on as a fraction.

> **Example question**: Change $\frac{25}{6}$ to a mixed number.
> $25 \div 6 = 4$ remainder 1. So the answer is $4\frac{1}{6}$.

Top tip!

Think of a fraction as a division sum using the line as the $\div$. Divide to find decimals, e.g. $\frac{1}{2} = 1 \div 2 = 0.5$

Listen up
9

Keywords

Fraction ➤ Any part of a number, e.g. $\frac{3}{4}$ means 3 out of 4 equal parts

Equivalent fractions ➤ Different fractions that represent the same amount

Reduce ➤ Simplify a fraction to get the lowest **numerator** and **denominator** possible

Improper fractions ➤ Any fraction where the **numerator** is bigger than the **denominator** – they are 'top-heavy' fractions, e.g. $\frac{10}{8}$

Mixed numbers ➤ Numbers that are a mix of integers and fractions, e.g. $4\frac{3}{5}$

Have a go!

Buy a packet of multi-coloured sweets. Sort them into colours. What fraction of the whole is each colour? Can you reduce any of these fractions?

Test yourself

1 Liu has a purse with eight copper and four silver coins in it only. What fraction are copper coins?

2 Complete this row of equivalent fractions.
$$\frac{1}{4} = \frac{\square}{12} = \frac{6}{\square} = \frac{\square}{48}$$

3 Reduce these fractions.
a. $\frac{10}{25}$ b. $\frac{18}{36}$ c. $\frac{14}{49}$

4 Change these improper fractions to mixed numbers.
a. $\frac{21}{8}$ b. $\frac{17}{5}$ c. $\frac{38}{9}$

Comparing fractions

Ordering or comparing fractions is easy where the **denominators** are the same.

For example: $\frac{7}{8} > \frac{5}{8} > \frac{3}{8}$

It's harder to compare fractions with different denominators. Remember your **multiples** and how to find **equivalent fractions**.

Example question: Put the correct symbol between these two fractions,

$\frac{3}{5} \square \frac{5}{7}$

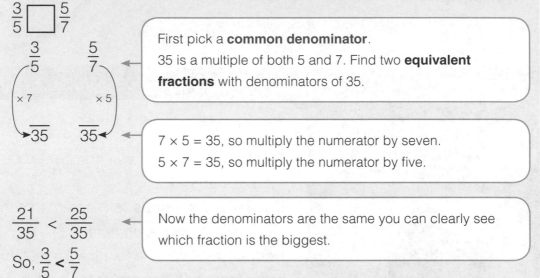

First pick a **common denominator**.

35 is a multiple of both 5 and 7. Find two **equivalent fractions** with denominators of 35.

$7 \times 5 = 35$, so multiply the numerator by seven.
$5 \times 7 = 35$, so multiply the numerator by five.

$\frac{21}{35} < \frac{25}{35}$

Now the denominators are the same you can clearly see which fraction is the biggest.

So, $\frac{3}{5} < \frac{5}{7}$

Adding and subtracting fractions

If the denominators are the same, add or subtract the numerators.

For example: $\frac{7}{10} + \frac{2}{10} = \frac{9}{10}$ $\qquad$ $\frac{7}{8} - \frac{3}{8} = \frac{4}{8}$

If the denominators are different, use equivalent fractions with **common denominators**.

Example question: Ellie, Jayna and Anisa share a chocolate bar. Ellie eats $\frac{1}{4}$, Jayna eats $\frac{3}{16}$ and Anisa eats $\frac{3}{8}$. What fraction of the chocolate bar is left?

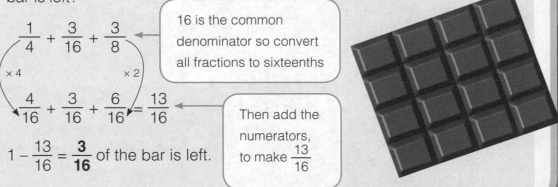

$\frac{1}{4} + \frac{3}{16} + \frac{3}{8}$

16 is the common denominator so convert all fractions to sixteenths

$\frac{4}{16} + \frac{3}{16} + \frac{6}{16} = \frac{13}{16}$

Then add the numerators, to make $\frac{13}{16}$

$1 - \frac{13}{16} = \frac{3}{16}$ of the bar is left.

Adding and subtracting fractions (continued)

You can add and subtract **mixed numbers** in the same way.
First, add the integers. Then add the fractions.
If you end up with an improper fraction, change it back to a mixed number and add it to the total.

For example:

$$4\frac{3}{5} + 2\frac{4}{5} = 6\frac{7}{5} = 7\frac{2}{5}$$

To find a common denominator, write multiples of each denominator until you find a common one.
For example:

$\frac{1}{③}$ → 6   9   ⑫   **Common Denominator**

$\frac{1}{④}$ → 8   ⑫

Top tip!

Keyword

Common denominator ➤ A denominator that is a multiple of all denominators in a calculation

Have a go!

Choose four cards from a pack of 1-9 digit cards. Use them to make two fractions.

➤ Compare fractions using
  <, > or =.
➤ Add the fractions.
➤ Find the difference between the fractions.

Test yourself

❶ Arrange these fractions from smallest to largest.
$\frac{2}{3}, \frac{1}{2}, \frac{5}{6}, \frac{1}{4}, \frac{7}{12}$

❷ Circle the largest fraction.
$\frac{3}{4}, \frac{10}{12}, \frac{7}{8}, \frac{2}{3}$

❸ Calculate:
a. $2\frac{3}{5} + 1\frac{1}{5}$ b. $\frac{3}{4} + \frac{1}{8}$

c. $\frac{3}{5} + \frac{1}{4}$

❹ Calculate:
a. $\frac{8}{9} - \frac{3}{9}$ b. $\frac{4}{5} - \frac{7}{10}$ c. $\frac{6}{7} - \frac{3}{4}$

Fractions of an amount

You can calculate **fractions of an amount**.

The easiest examples to work out are those using **unit fractions**.

Example question: What is $\frac{1}{3}$ of £3.75?

$$3 \overline{\smash{)}£3.7^1 5} = £1.25$$

> Divide the amount by the denominator. £3.75 ÷ 3

$\frac{1}{3}$ of £3.75 is **£1.25**

> You could use **short division**.

Non-unit fractions are two-step problems.

Start in the same way as **unit fractions**.

Example question: What is $\frac{3}{5}$ of 985?

$$5 \overline{\smash{)}9^4 8^3 5} = 197$$

> Divide 985 by five to find $\frac{1}{5}$.

$$\begin{array}{r} 197 \\ \times \quad 3 \\ \hline 591 \\ {\scriptstyle 2\ 2} \end{array}$$

> You now know $\frac{1}{5}$. Multiply 197 by three to find $\frac{3}{5}$.

$\frac{3}{5}$ of 985 = **591**

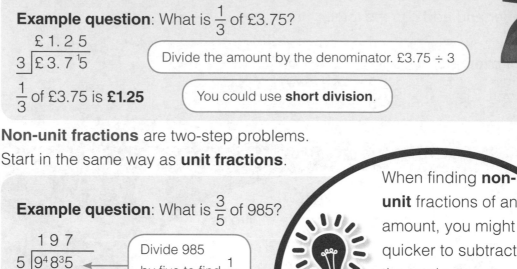

When finding **non-unit** fractions of an amount, you might find it quicker to subtract from the total amount. For example, with $\frac{4}{5}$ of 25, it's quicker to subtract $\frac{1}{5}$ from 25 than to find $\frac{1}{5}$ of 25 and multiply.

Sometimes, rather than finding a fraction of the amount, you might have to work backwards to find the **whole** amount.

Example question: $\frac{3}{8}$ of a magazine contains pages with adverts. 36 pages are adverts. How many pages are there in the magazine?

You know that three-eighths of the total number of pages is 36.

$\frac{3}{8}$ of the magazine = 36 pages

Divide 36 by three to find out what one-eighth is.

36 ÷ 3 = 12. One-eighth = 12.

If one-eighth is 12 then the whole magazine, or eight eighths, is eight times that amount.

$\frac{8}{8}$ of the magazine = 8 × 12 = 96.

So the magazine has **96 pages**.

Multiplying and dividing fractions

Fractions can be shown as a number sentence, e.g. two-fifths of twenty can be written as $\frac{2}{5} \times 20$

But what if you have to multiply two fractions together? Multiply the numerators and denominators together to make a new fraction.

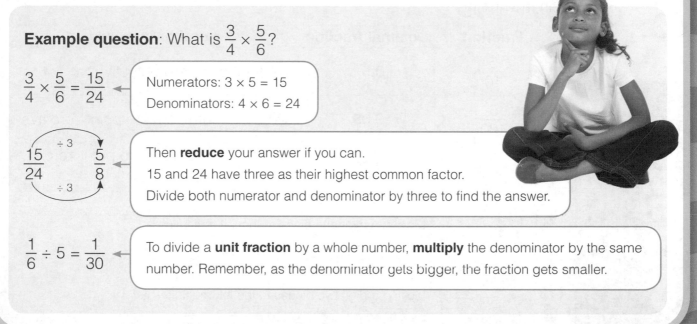

Example question: What is $\frac{3}{4} \times \frac{5}{6}$?

$\frac{3}{4} \times \frac{5}{6} = \frac{15}{24}$

Numerators: $3 \times 5 = 15$
Denominators: $4 \times 6 = 24$

$\frac{15}{24} \xrightarrow{\div 3} \frac{5}{8}$

Then **reduce** your answer if you can.
15 and 24 have three as their highest common factor.
Divide both numerator and denominator by three to find the answer.

$\frac{1}{6} \div 5 = \frac{1}{30}$

To divide a **unit fraction** by a whole number, **multiply** the denominator by the same number. Remember, as the denominator gets bigger, the fraction gets smaller.

Keywords

Fractions of an amount ➤ If you divide a quantity, total or size into equal parts then these are fractions of that amount

Unit fraction ➤ Any fraction with a **numerator** of one

Non-unit fraction ➤ Any fraction with a numerator greater than one

Listen up 11

Have a go!

Fold a sheet of paper into halves, quarters and then eighths. Unfold the paper and write the number four in each section.

Refold the paper to show how $\frac{2}{8}$ of 32 is 8, $\frac{4}{8}$ is 16, $\frac{6}{8}$ is 24 and $\frac{8}{8}$ is 32.

Repeat with other numbers.

Test yourself

① Calculate:
  a. $\frac{1}{5}$ of 850   c. $\frac{1}{3}$ of £6.48
  b. $\frac{2}{3}$ of 1500 ml   d. $\frac{3}{4}$ of 468

② In a class of children, 18 children have packed lunches. $\frac{1}{4}$ of the children have school dinners. All children eat at school. How many children are there in the class?

③ Calculate:
  a. $\frac{3}{8} \times 48 =$ c. $\frac{2}{3} \times \frac{2}{3} =$
  b. $\frac{1}{3} \div 3 =$ d. $\frac{1}{4} \div 5 =$

Decimal place value

0.08

As with whole numbers, the position of the digit in the decimal shows its value. This is known as **place value**. The value of the five digits in these **decimal fractions** depends on its place in the number.

Fraction	Decimal fraction	Number in words
$\frac{5}{10}$	0.**5**	five-tenths or zero point five
$\frac{5}{100}$	0.0**5**	five-hundredths or zero point zero five
$\frac{5}{1000}$	0.00**5**	five-thousandths or zero point zero zero five

0 . 0 3 7
0 . 3 7

> Moving a digit one place to the left multiplies it by ten. 0.037 × 10 = 0.37

0 . 0 3 7
3 . 7

> Moving a digit two places to the left multiplies it by a hundred. 0.037 × 100 = 3.7

3 . 7
0 . 3 7

> Moving a digit one place to the right divides it by ten. 3.7 ÷ 10 = 0.37

3 . 7
0 . 0 3 7

> Moving a digit two places to the right divides it by a hundred. 3.7 ÷ 100 = 0.037

Keywords

Decimal fraction ➤ Any fraction where the denominator is a power of 10; they are often just called **decimals**

Decimal places ➤ Decides how accurate a decimal answer is, e.g. a decimal rounded to one decimal place will be rounded to the nearest tenth. 3.78 → 3.8

Listen up
12

Parent tip!

Children are often taught to multiply a number by 10 or 100 by adding one or two zeros at the end. This does not work for decimals, e.g. 3.4 × 10 = 34 not 3.40. What really happens is the digits move to the left.

Comparing and rounding decimals

To compare decimals, look at the digits in the largest **place value** position. If these are the same, look at the value of the digits to the right. Keep doing this until you have found the larger number.

Example question: Put these decimals in order.

As they all have 3 in the ones position, look at the **tenths** digit.

3.**0**8 is the only number without any **tenths** so cross it off as the smallest.

3.**18** and 3.**12**8 both have one in the **tenths** position so look at the **hundredths**.

3.**18** is bigger.

The remaining numbers can all be ordered by the **tenths** digit with 3.**8** as the biggest.

Answer:

Like all numbers, decimals are easier to work with when **rounded**. You may be asked to write decimal answers rounded to a number of **decimal places**. This is especially important with money, which is rounded to two **decimal places**. That's the same as the nearest hundredth of a pound or the nearest penny.

Example question: On three visits to the filling station, Beth bought 25.628 litres, 17.432 litres and 20.516 litres of diesel. How many litres has she bought altogether? Round your answer to two decimal places.

First add the three decimal numbers using a column method. Remember to line up the columns. The total is **63.576 litres**.

To round, look at the second **decimal place**.
The digit to the right is **6** so round up the hundredths digit to 8.
Include the units of measurement in your answer: **63.58 litres**

6 3.5⑦6 → 6 3.5 8 ←

Shopping receipts and petrol prices are great contexts for practising decimals.

➤ Based on the receipt for one week's shopping, what would your bill be for ten weeks?

➤ How much would ten litres of unleaded petrol cost?

1 A mouse weighs one hundred times less than a cat. The cat weighs 4.25 kg. How much does the mouse weigh?

2 Put these lengths in order, starting with the smallest.

8.1 cm, 8.08 cm, 8.081 cm, 8.9 cm, 8.81 cm

Decimal / fraction equivalents

Decimal fractions are easier to work with than fractions. You probably know some decimal fraction equivalents, for example $\frac{1}{2} = 0.5$ and $\frac{1}{10} = 0.1$

To convert a fraction to its decimal equivalent, divide the **numerator** by the **denominator**.

Example question: Convert $\frac{5}{8}$ to a decimal fraction.

Calculate $5 \div 8$. First make an **estimate** of your answer. $\frac{4}{8} = \frac{1}{2}$ which is 0.5, so $\frac{5}{8}$ is going to be a little bigger.

Use **long division**.

```
    0. 6
8 ) 5. 0 0
    4. 8 ↓
       2 0
```

Set your numbers out neatly in digits.

8 goes into 50 six times because $6 \times 8 = 48$.

Subtract 48 from 50. 'Bring down' a zero from above.

Form a new division, $20 \div 8$.

```
    0. 6 2 5
8 ) 5. 0 0 0
    4. 8 ↓
       2 0
       1 6 ↓
         4 0
```

8 goes into 20 two times because $2 \times 8 = 16$.

Subtract 16 from 20.

'Bring down' a zero from above. Form the next step, $40 \div 8$.

Finally 8 goes into 40 five times.

$\frac{5}{8}$ = **0.625** as a decimal fraction. That's a little bigger than 0.5 so it fits with the estimate.

With some decimal fractions you will never reach the end of the answer. A decimal fraction like this is called a **recurring decimal**. There is no end to this operation so you have to decide when to stop. You might round to two decimal places or show that the decimal recurs with a symbol.

Example question: Convert $\frac{5}{9}$ to a decimal fraction.

```
    0. 5 5 5
9 ) 5. 0 0 0
    4 5 ↓
      5 0
      4 5 ↓
        5 0
```

9 goes into 50 five times because $5 \times 9 = 45$. But you always have 5 left over.

'Bringing down' a zero makes the same division again.

So $\frac{5}{9}$ as a decimal is **0.56** rounded to two decimal places or **0.5̇**

Fractions, decimals and percentages

Parts of a whole can be written either as a fraction, a decimal fraction or a percentage **(FDP)**.

Look at these different ways of showing a quarter.

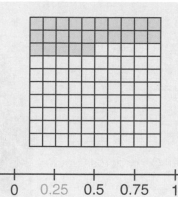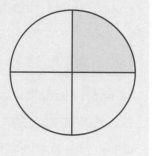

To convert a decimal fraction to a **percentage**, multiply by 100: $0.75 \times 100 = 75\%$

To convert a **percentage** to a decimal fraction, divide by 100: $60\% \div 100 = 0.6$ (six-tenths)

Keywords

Recurring decimal ➤ Decimals that have a repeating digit or pattern of digits, for example $\frac{1}{3}$ can be shown as $0.\dot{3}$

FDP ➤ Fraction, decimal and percentage. Three different ways of showing the same part of a quantity, total or size

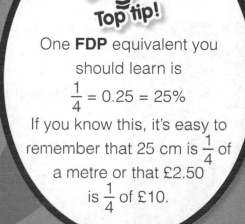

Top tip!

One **FDP** equivalent you should learn is
$$\frac{1}{4} = 0.25 = 25\%$$
If you know this, it's easy to remember that 25 cm is $\frac{1}{4}$ of a metre or that £2.50 is $\frac{1}{4}$ of £10.

Have a go!

Play 'Kim's Game' or 'pairs' with fraction/decimal equivalents.

Write out 16 cards with the fractions $\frac{1}{2}, \frac{1}{3}, \frac{1}{4}, \frac{1}{5}, \frac{1}{6}, \frac{1}{8}, \frac{1}{9}$ and $\frac{1}{10}$ and their decimal fraction equivalents, 0.5, 0.333, 0.25, 0.2, 0.167, 0.125, 0.111 and 0.1.

Turn them face down in a 4 × 4 grid and take turns to find matching pairs.

Test yourself

❶ Convert $\frac{3}{8}$ to a decimal fraction.

❷ Convert $\frac{7}{20}$ to a decimal fraction.

❸ $\frac{6}{7}$ as a decimal fraction is 0.8571429. Round it to two decimal places.

❹ What is 0.75 as a percentage and a fraction?

❺ What is 55.5% as a decimal fraction?

Multiplying decimals

You use decimal numbers every day. Pounds and pence and measures such as length, weight, area and capacity are all decimal numbers. As with whole numbers you can use short or long multiplication.

Example question: Amar and five friends visit a theme park. The entrance cost is £18.95 each. How much will it cost them altogether?

Make an estimate. £18.95 is pretty close to £20. £20 × 6 = £120.

```
  £ 1 8.9 5
×         6
  £ 1 1 3.7 0
    5  5  3
```

Use **short multiplication**. £18.95 × 6.

Start with the hundredths column. Carry across any tenths that you make. Make a note of them below the line. Add them to the total when you multiply that column by 6. Continue with each column.

The answer of **£113.70** is close to the estimate of £120.

Use **long multiplication** to multiply decimals by two-digit numbers. Making an estimate is even more important when dealing with bigger numbers.

Example question: A fence panel is 3.23 m long. A builder uses 24 panels to build a fence. How long will the fence be?

3.23 rounded to the nearest metre is 3 m. 24 is close to 25.

3 m × 25 = 75 m. So you are expecting your answer to be about 75 m.

```
  3.2 3
×   2 4
  1 2.9 2
```

Partition 24 into 20 + 4 and do two sets of multiplication.

Start with 3.23 × 4. Use **short multiplication**. Carry any tenths, ones or tens you make into the next column.

```
  3.2 3
×   2 4
  1 2.9 2
  6 4.6 0
  7 7.5 2
```

Next multiply 3.23 by 20. You are multiplying by a multiple of ten, 20. Place a zero in the ones column before you start.

Use column addition to arrive at the answer, **77.52 m** which is close to your estimate. Don't forget to include **units of measurement** in your answer.

Dividing decimals

You can use standard methods with decimals in the same way as whole numbers.

Example question: Jag buys four cans of cola for £1.88. Karl buys eight cans for £3.44. Karl says that he has paid less for each can. Is he right? Show how you know.

For this type of problem you will need to use **reasoning**. It is not enough to say that Karl is right. You must prove it.

Start by dividing each multipack to find the cost of one can.

Jag

```
  0. 4 7
4 1. 8 ²8
```

£1.88 ÷ 4 has been completed **using short division**. £3.44 ÷ 8 is shown with a **long division** method.
You could use either standard method.

Karl

```
  0. 4 3
8 3. 4 4
  3. 2 ↓
    2 4
```

Karl is right. Show the two divisions in your answer. Also state clearly that Jag's cans cost £0.47 or 47p each whereas Karl's cans cost £0.43 or 43p.

Top tip! When writing amounts of money use only one symbol. So £2.50 and 250p are correct but £2.50p is not.

Keywords

Unit of measurement ➤ A quantity used as a standard of measurement

Reasoning ➤ Explaining and justifying your answer, e.g. by showing how you know that something is correct

Listen up **14**

Have a go! On your next trip to the supermarket look out for some multipacks of drinks or tinned food.

Calculate the price of each item in the multipack to see whether you are getting a good deal.

Test yourself

❶ Calculate 4.67 × 4

❷ A builder lays eight paving slabs end to end. Each one is 1.14 m long. How long will they be together?

❸ Calculate £7.92 ÷ 3

❹ Lucy buys a boxed set of five novels for £18.75. If she bought them individually they would cost £3.95 each. How much does she save?

This mind map will help you remember all the main points from this topic. Have a go at drawing your own mind map.

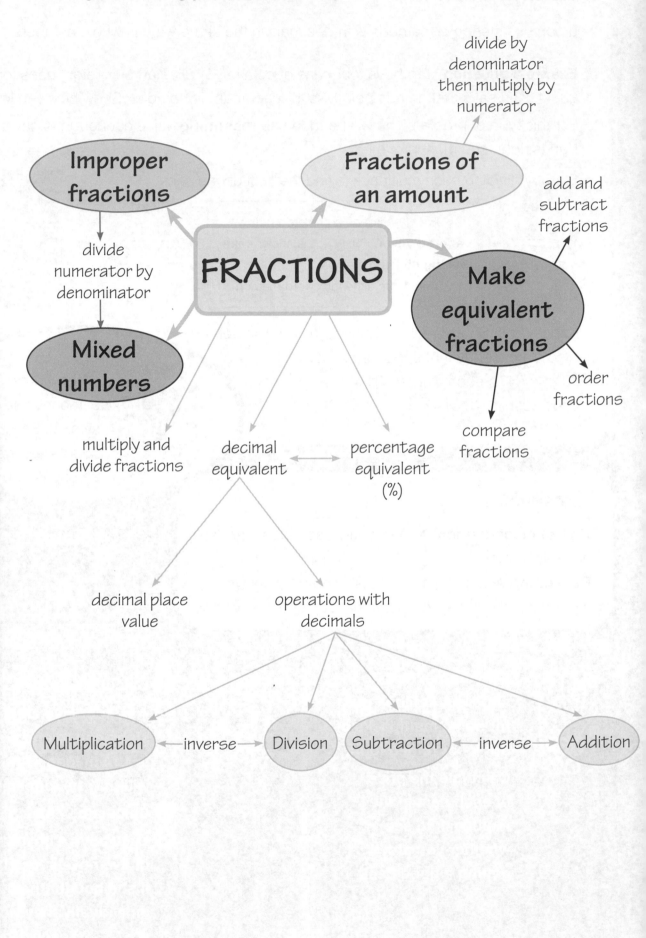

Fractions, Decimals, Percentages

1 Complete these equivalent fraction pairs. **(3 marks)**

a. $\dfrac{3}{4} = \dfrac{\square}{8}$ b. $\dfrac{10}{12} = \dfrac{\square}{6}$ c. $\dfrac{15}{\square} = \dfrac{5}{9}$

2 Change these improper fractions to mixed numbers. Reduce your answer if you can. **(3 marks)**

a. $\dfrac{20}{6}$ ....   b. $\dfrac{27}{4}$ ....   c. $\dfrac{56}{9}$ ....

3 Calculate the following. **(4 marks)**

a. $\dfrac{2}{3} + \dfrac{1}{12} = \square$ b. $\dfrac{4}{5} - \dfrac{2}{3} = \square$

c. $\dfrac{1}{12} \div 2 = \square$ d. $\dfrac{2}{3} \times \dfrac{3}{6} = \square$

4 $\dfrac{3}{13}$ of the 26 children in Class 6T wear glasses. How many is this? **(1 mark)**

....

5 Kell saves $\dfrac{1}{4}$ of his pocket money. In four weeks he saves £5.80. How much pocket money does Kell get each week? **(1 mark)**

....

6 Draw lines to match the fractions to their decimal or percentage equivalents.

$\dfrac{3}{4}$ $\dfrac{40}{100}$ $\dfrac{3}{8}$ $\dfrac{3}{5}$

0.4   60%   0.375   75%   **(4 marks)**

7 Arrange these decimal numbers from smallest to largest. **(1 mark)**

0.7617, 0.7, 0.7771, 0.78, 0.81, 0.0977

....

8 Ten friends equally share £34635. How much does each one receive? **(1 mark)**

....

9 Shams buys twelve 1.5 litre bottles of cola. How much cola does he have? **(1 mark)**

....

10 Calculate 347.8 ÷ 4 **(1 mark)**

....

Proportion

Ratio and **proportion** are two ways of describing parts of an amount. From mixing the right ratio of sand and cement when making concrete to measuring distances on a map, these are important maths skills.

Example question: The proportion of children who wear glasses in Mr Brown's class is two in every seven. There are 28 children in Mr Brown's class. How many of them wear glasses?

The proportion who wear glasses is two out of every seven or $\frac{2}{7}$.

There are 28 children in the class. $28 \div 7 = 4$ groups of seven children.

In each of these four groups, two children will be wearing glasses. $4 \times 2 = 8$

There are **eight children** who wear glasses.

You might have to describe a pattern or a situation as a proportion.

Example question: In Miss Shah's class there are 32 children. Eight wear glasses. What proportion of the children wear glasses?

You know that the proportion who wear glasses is eight in every 32 or $\frac{8}{32}$.

Reduce or **simplify** this fraction to make it easier to understand.

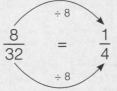

$$\frac{8}{32} = \frac{1}{4}$$

The proportion of children who wear glasses is one in every four or $\frac{1}{4}$.

Keywords

Ratio ➤ Compares parts of the whole amount, e.g. the ratio of red to white cars is three to four. You can write this as a ratio, 3:4

Proportion ➤ A part of an amount compared to the whole, e.g. the proportion of white cars is one in every five. You can write this as a fraction, $\frac{1}{5}$

Simplify ➤ Divide both numbers in a fraction, ratio or proportion by the same number to make them easier to understand

Ratio

A ratio compares parts of a whole. The whole might get bigger or smaller but the relationship between the parts stays the same.

Example question: When making cookies, the ratio of flour to butter to sugar is 3:2:1. Kit is baking a batch of cookies and uses 900g of ingredients. How much of this is butter?

When solving this type of question, write out a table to help you with the different amounts.

Flour	Butter	Sugar	Total
3	2	1	6
450g	300g	150g	900g

Divide the total, 900g, by the total of all parts in the ratio, 6.
900g ÷ 6 = 150g

You can now complete the table and see that Kit has used 300g of butter.

Top tip! Proportion is another way of dealing with fractions of an amount. Ratio compares the parts of that amount together.

Listen up
15

Have a go! Look up some popular recipes for fruit smoothies.

Can you reduce the amounts of each ingredient to a ratio?

Create your own smoothie according to a ratio of your favourite ingredients.

Test yourself

1. Four children in a class of 32 have a dog. What proportion is this?

2. Li Yan is half the weight of her mother. Together they weigh 90 kg. How much does Li Yan weigh?

3. In a bag there are three red marbles for every five blue marbles. There are 48 marbles in the bag. How many of them are blue?

4. Two numbers are in the ratio 1:4. One of the numbers is 12. The other number could be one of two possible values. What are they?

Percentages of an amount

You need to be able to calculate a **percentage** of a quantity.

You can find 10 percent or one **tenth** of any quantity by dividing it by 10. Move the digits one place to the right, e.g. 10% of £34.00 = £34.00 ÷ 10 = £3.40

You can find 1 percent or one **hundredth** of any quantity by dividing it by one hundred. Move the digits two places to the right, e.g. 1% of £34.00 = £34.00 ÷ 100 = £0.34

By adding blocks of 10 percent and 1 percent you can calculate any percentage of any amount.

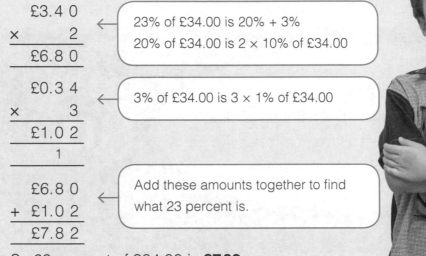

Example question: What is 23 percent of £34.00?

```
  £3.4 0
×       2
  £6.8 0
```
23% of £34.00 is 20% + 3%
20% of £34.00 is 2 × 10% of £34.00

```
  £0.3 4
×       3
  £1.0 2
      1
```
3% of £34.00 is 3 × 1% of £34.00

```
  £6.8 0
+ £1.0 2
  £7.8 2
```
Add these amounts together to find what 23 percent is.

So 23 percent of £34.00 is **£7.82**

Parent tip!

Encourage your child to find short cuts when calculating percentages. For example 9 percent can be calculated by finding 10 percent and subtracting 1 percent. To find 25 percent halve the amount to find 50 percent and then halve it again.

Keywords

Percentage ➤ A fraction out of 100. It is usually shown using the % symbol or 'percent'

Increasing ➤ Making an amount larger

Decreasing ➤ Making an amount smaller

Listen up 16

Raising and lowering prices

You can work out price cuts and price rises when you know how to calculate percentages.

Increasing and **decreasing** prices are two-step problems. First, work out the percentage. Second, either add it to, or subtract it from, the original price.

Example question: A tablet computer that costs £279 is reduced in price by 15 percent. What is the new price?

10% of £279 = £279 ÷ 10 = £27.90
5% of £279 = half of 10%.   £27.90 ÷ 2 = £13.95
15% of £279 = £27.90 + £13.95 = £41.85

> First calculate 15 percent of £279. Find blocks of 10 percent and 5 percent and add them together.

£279 – £41.85 = £237.15 ← Then subtract 15 percent from the original price.
The new price is **£237.15**

You can use standard methods for any of the addition, subtraction and division operations you need to complete here.

Example question: Mr Huang has a bill for £85. If he doesn't pay it within 30 days it will **increase** by 5%. How much will the new bill be?

5% = half of 10%. ← First calculate 5 percent of £85.
10% of £85 = £85 ÷ 10 = £8.50
£8.50 ÷ 2 = £4.25, so 5 percent is £4.25

£85 + £4.25 = £89.25 ← Then add 5 percent to the original bill of £85.
The new bill is **£89.25**.

Have a go!

When shopping look for any offers that use percentage.

For example, if a breakfast cereal offers 10 percent extra or a price has been reduced by 20 percent, use your maths to check that the deal is right.

Test yourself

1. What is 30 percent of 240 m?
2. Jeans that cost £18 are reduced by 10 percent. How much do they cost now?
3. A monthly energy bill of £175 increases by 6 percent. How much is the new bill?

Scale

Builders, designers and architects all use **scale** plans, maps, models and drawings. If you understand how to use scale, you can solve problems with shapes and distances on maps.

Similar shapes

Look at these three triangles.

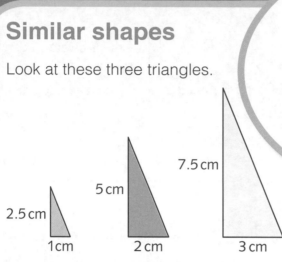

2.5 cm

5 cm

7.5 cm

1 cm   2 cm   3 cm

Top tip!

Drawings in test questions might not be **drawn to scale**. This means that there is no relationship between the measurements in the drawing and the actual size of the object.

The **ratio** between the width and height of each triangle is the same so they are all **similar** triangles.

Example question: What would be the width of a similar triangle that was 20 cm high?

The ratio of width to height is 1:2.5
The height is always two-and-a-half times the width. Use the **inverse** operation. Divide the height by two-and-a-half to find the width.
20 ÷ 2.5 = 8.
A triangle with a height of 20 cm would be **8 cm wide**.

Keywords

Scale ➤ Scaling something means that you reduce or enlarge all of its dimensions. The scale of a map or drawing means the ratio between the measurements on the model or drawing and the size of the actual object or distance

Similar ➤ Shapes that are the same shape as each other but not the same size

Scale factor ➤ A ratio that shows the amount of enlargement or a ratio between two sets of measurements

Scale factor

Shapes and other objects can increase or decrease in size according to a ratio or **scale factor**.

Example question: Erik has a model train set with a **scale factor** of 1:76. His model locomotive is 28 cm long. How long would the actual locomotive be?

From the **scale factor** you know that the actual locomotive is 76 times larger than the model.
Use long multiplication or the grid method to calculate the answer.
28 × 76 = 2128 cm.
The actual locomotive would be **21.28 m long**.

Distances

In a map or a scale drawing, the scale is the ratio between the distance on the map or drawing and the actual measurement of the original.

Example question: On a map with a scale of 1:5000, two locations are 3.5 cm apart. How far are the actual locations apart in metres?

One centimetre on the map represents 5000 cm on the ground.
Multiply 3.5 by 5000 to find out how far apart the locations are.
3.5 cm × 5000 = 17 500 cm
Convert the centimetres to the units you have been asked to give your answer in.
1 m = 100 cm so divide your answer by 100. 17 500 ÷ 100 = 175
The locations are **175 m apart**.

Try creating a scale plan of your bedroom. Record how it appears now or create a design of how you would like it to be.

❶ Draw three similar rectangles that have a length that is double their width.

❷ On a 1:200 scale model of a pirate ship, the mast is 9 cm tall. How tall is the actual mast in metres?

❸ Two locations are 3 cm apart on a 1:25 000 scale map. How many metres is this?

Steps to solve problems

There are several steps you can take to help you solve a problem.

1 Read the problem and try to picture it. You could:
- circle or highlight the key words and numbers
- draw a picture

2 Choose a calculation. There might be more than one step. Maybe make an **estimate**.

3 Check the answer:
- Does it make sense?
- Use the **inverse** operation to check it.
- Have you used the correct **units of measurement**?

Example question 1: At Fern Valley Primary School there are 300 children. 35 percent walk to school and 55 percent come by car. How many more children come by car than walk?

Highlight the important numbers and words. This shows that it is a two-step problem.

First, use the percentages to find the numbers of children who come by car and who walk.

Then find the difference between these numbers. 'How many more ... than' tells you to use subtraction.

Make an **estimate**. 35 percent is about a third and 55 percent is close to a half so your answers should be around 100 children who walk and around 150 who arrive by car.

35 percent of 300 = 105   ←   Find percentages
55 percent of 300 = 165
165 – 105 = 60   ←   Subtraction

So there are 60 more children who come by car than walk.

Steps to solve problems (continued)

Example question 2: Pick 'n' Mix sweets cost 70p for 100 g. Freya bought a bag of sweets for £1.75. How many grams of sweets did she buy?

You could draw a picture to help you. You know that 70p is enough for a 100 g bag of sweets. How many bags of 100 g can be bought for £1.75?

If you draw and label two 100 g bags that together cost £1.40 you can see that there is 35p left over. This is enough for half of a 100 g bag or 50 g.

So Freya has bought 100 g + 100 g + 50 g = **250 g of sweets.**

As well as helping you to solve a problem, writing down your working out and making jottings could earn you marks, even if your final answer is incorrect.

Top tip!

Have a go!

Find or make up an acronym to help you remember the steps to solve problems. For example RUCSAC (Read, Underline, Calculation, Solve, Answer, Check).

Test yourself

❶ Lane End Primary School has 312 students. They want to double the number of students that walk to school from one in every six to one in every three. If they do, how many more children will walk to school?

❷ Sara bought a 160 g bag of Fruit Drops and Jelly Beans. Three out of every five sweets in the bag is a Fruit Drop. What is the weight of Jelly Beans in the bag?

This mind map will help you remember all the main points from this topic. Have a go at drawing your own mind map.

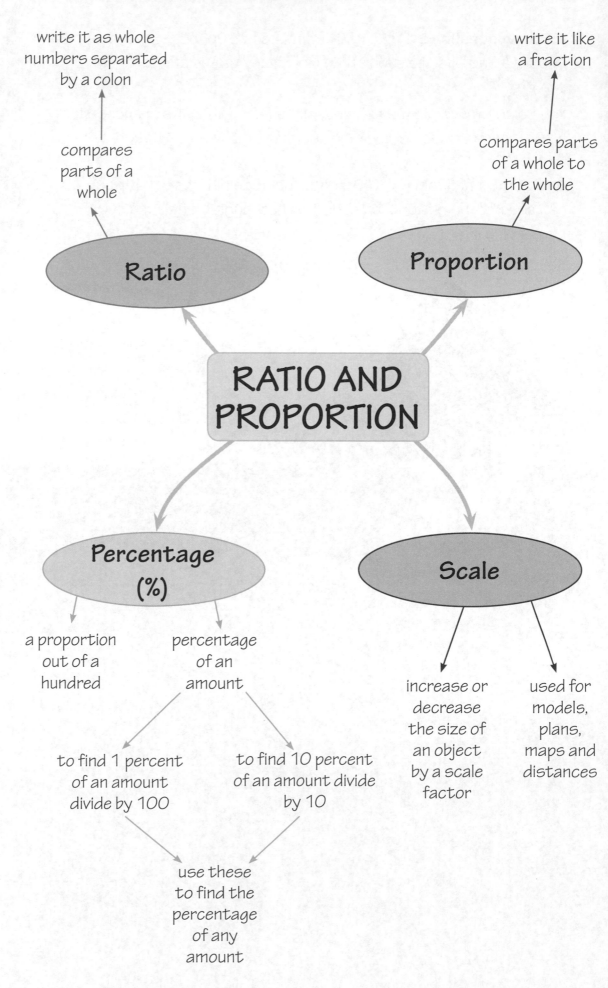

write it as whole
numbers separated
by a colon

compares
parts of a
whole

Ratio

RATIO AND PROPORTION

Proportion

write it like
a fraction

compares parts
of a whole to
the whole

Percentage
(%)

a proportion
out of a
hundred

percentage
of an
amount

to find 1 percent
of an amount
divide by 100

to find 10 percent
of an amount divide
by 10

use these
to find the
percentage
of any
amount

Scale

increase or
decrease
the size of
an object
by a scale
factor

used for
models,
plans,
maps and
distances

1 In Miss Patel's class, one in every eight children is left-handed.
There are 32 children in the class. How many are left-handed? **(1 mark)**

....

2 In a tin of sweets, the ratio of orange to cola to lime sweets is 3:5:4
There are 204 sweets in the tin. How many are there of each flavour? **(1 mark)**

....

3 Look at this pattern. **(1 mark)**
Colour more squares until the ratio of shaded to unshaded squares is 3:1

4 Calculate:

   a. 10 percent of £35.60 = ... **(1 mark)**

   b. 45 percent of 1240 = ... **(1 mark)**

5 Carla works on Saturday at the hairdressers. She was paid £26. Her wages
have just increased by 20 percent. How much does she get paid now?
(1 mark)

....

6 On this grid draw a similar triangle that is three times smaller. **(1 mark)**

7 On a 1:50 000 scale map, a distance is measured as being 15 cm.
How far would this actually be in kilometres? **(1 mark)**

....

8 At Roman Road Primary School, 90 percent of the infant children have school
meals. That is twice the proportion of junior children. There are 120 infants
and 220 juniors in the school. How many children in total have school meals?
(1 mark)

....

Missing numbers

Finding the missing number in a calculation involves using **algebra**.

If you know some numbers in a missing number question, you can use them to find the missing number. Remember to use **inverse operations**.

Examples:

$\boxed{} \div 12 = 15$

The **inverse** of division is multiplication. Calculate $15 \times 12 =$ **180**

$4 \times \boxed{} = 272$

The **inverse** of multiplication is division. Calculate $272 \div 4 =$ **68**

$243.6 - \boxed{} = 102.5$

With the missing number in this position, use subtraction to find the answer. $243.6 - 102.5 =$ **141.1**

$8\frac{1}{2} + \boxed{} = 10$

The **inverse** of addition is subtraction.
$10 - 8\frac{1}{2} = \mathbf{1\frac{1}{2}}$

You can check your answer by completing the operation after you have slotted in the missing number. Do both sides of the equals sign balance?

Where there is more than one missing value, there may be more than one correct answer.

Example question: What could the two missing numbers be?

$\boxed{} \times 6 = 150 - \boxed{}$

Balance the equation by making both sides of the equals sign have the same value. For example $20 \times 6 = 150 - 30$ or $10 \times 6 = 150 - 90$.

Top tip! In calculations where you subtract or divide whole numbers, the biggest number will need to come first. In calculations where you multiply or add whole numbers, the biggest number will come at the end.

Missing angles and lengths

You might have to find other missing values such as **angles** and measurements.

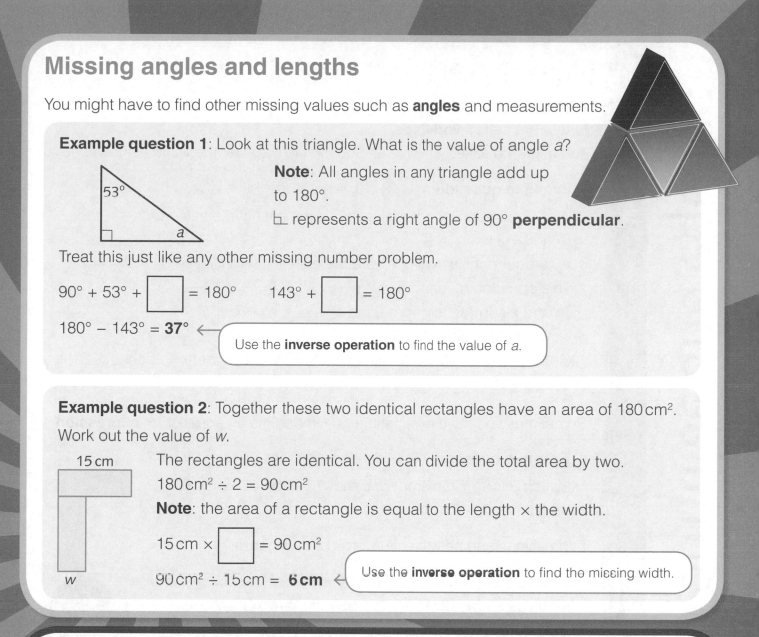

Example question 1: Look at this triangle. What is the value of angle *a*?

Note: All angles in any triangle add up to 180°.

⌐ represents a right angle of 90° **perpendicular**.

Treat this just like any other missing number problem.

$90° + 53° + \boxed{} = 180°$ $143° + \boxed{} = 180°$

$180° - 143° = \mathbf{37°}$ ← Use the **inverse operation** to find the value of *a*.

Example question 2: Together these two identical rectangles have an area of 180 cm². Work out the value of *w*.

The rectangles are identical. You can divide the total area by two.

$180\,cm^2 \div 2 = 90\,cm^2$

Note: the area of a rectangle is equal to the length × the width.

$15\,cm \times \boxed{} = 90\,cm^2$

$90\,cm^2 \div 15\,cm = \mathbf{6\,cm}$ ← Use the **inverse operation** to find the missing width.

Keywords

Algebra ➤ Maths where numbers or values are represented by letters or symbols

Angle ➤ The amount of turn between two straight lines that are joined at a point

Perpendicular ➤ Lines that are at a right angle (90°) to each other

Have a go! Choose three related numbers and make all four possible calculations. For example with 36, 9 and 4 you could make:
$4 \times 9 = 36$; $9 \times 4 = 36$;
$36 \div 4 = 9$; $36 \div 9 = 4$.

Test yourself

❶ Find the missing number.
a. $42.5 + \boxed{} = 83.8$
b. $\boxed{} - 62 = 438$
c. $360 \div \boxed{} = 45$
d. $\boxed{} \times 9 = 243$

❷ Calculate the value of angle *w*.

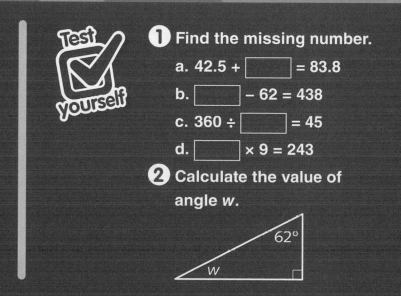

Equations and expressions

Equations in algebra use symbols or letters instead of empty boxes. These letters are called **variables**.

You might be asked to solve an equation to discover the value of the variable.

Example question: $x + 7 = 10$. What is the value of x?

When you add 7 to x it makes 10 so x must have a value of 3.

$5x + 6 = 21$

A number right in front of a **variable** means it is multiplied by that number. This equation means '5 times $x + 6 = 21$'.

To find x subtract six from each side of the equation.

Now consider $5x = 15$

Once you know that '5 times $x = 15$' you can see that $x = 3$ because $15 \div 5 = 3$.

Sometimes you have to substitute a number into an equation or **expression**.

Example question: What is the value of $8y + 6$ when $y = 7$?

Switch y for a 7 remembering that $8y$ means '8 times y'.

So 8 times $7 + 6 = 62$.

Expressions can be written in words or as **algebra**.

Example question: Jenny receives £y pocket money. George receives £2 more. George's pocket money $= y + 2$.

a. What expression describes Katy, who receives twice as much as Jenny?

$2y$

b. Or Junaid, who receives £2 less than Jenny?

$y - 2$

Keywords

Equation ➤ Uses an equals sign to separate two expressions with the same value, e.g. $2x = 10$ or $5 \times 3 = 10 + 5$

Variable ➤ A value in an equation that is represented by a symbol or letter

Expression ➤ Numbers, symbols and operation signs ($\times$, $\div$, $+$ and $-$) grouped together to show the value of something, e.g. $2 + 3$ or $7y + 3$

Formulae ➤ Rules that show the relationship between different **variables** – usually written as **equations**

Formulae

A **formula** shows the relationship between two or more **variables**.

An Olympic swimming pool has a length (*l*) of 50 m and a width (*w*) of 25 m.
The formula that describes the **area** of the pool (*a*) is $a = lw$.
$1250\,m^2 = 50\,m \times 25\,m$

The pool is filled with water to a depth (*d*) of 2 m. The formula that describes the **volume** of the pool (*v*) is $v = lwd$.
$2500\,m^3 = 50\,m \times 25\,m \times 2\,m$

The value of these variables might change but the relationship between them stays the same.

A football pitch that is 100 m long (*l*) and 60 m wide (*w*) has an area (*a*) of 6000 m². $a = lw$
$6000\,m^2 = 100\,m \times 60\,m$

A paddling pool that is 2.5 m long (*l*),
1 m wide (*w*) and 0.5 m deep (*d*) has
a volume of 1.25 m³. $v = lwd$
$1.25\,m^3 = 2.5\,m \times 1\,m \times 0.5\,m$

Top tip!

The multiplication symbol is not used in algebra as it could get confused with *x* used as a **variable**. For division you use a horizontal line, for example: $\frac{x}{2}$

Have a go!

Use algebra to predict your or a friend's height in centimetres as an adult. You need to know the father's height *x* and mother's height *y*.

For girls the expression is:
$\frac{x + y}{2} - 6.5$

For boys the expression is:
$\frac{x + y}{2} + 6.5$

Remember this is only a prediction!

Test yourself

1. What is the value of *x* in these equations?
   a. $4x = 12$
   b. $x + 9 = 45$
   c. $3x + 9 = 30$

2. If *t* equals 4, what is the value of:
   a. $5t - 6$ b. $\frac{t}{2} + 7$ c. $t^2 + 12$

3. There are *p* cars in the car park. Thirteen leave.

   Write an expression for the number of cars in the car park now.

Number sequences

Questions about number sequences usually ask you to continue the sequence or complete any gaps. **Linear number sequences** either increase or decrease by the same amount each time so to answer either type of question you will need to work out the **common difference** between each **term**.

Example question: What are the next three **terms** in this sequence?

28, 37, 46, 55, __, __, __

Decide whether the terms are increasing or decreasing and by how much.

They are increasing by **nine** each time. Write the next three terms.

28, 37, 46, 55, **64**, **73**, **82**

Remember the terms might be fractions or decimal numbers and they might get smaller as well as bigger each time.

Example question: Write the missing numbers in this sequence.

$16, 14\frac{1}{2}, \_\_, \_\_, 10, \_\_, 7, \_\_$

The difference between the first two terms in the sequence is $1\frac{1}{2}$. You can use this to calculate the four missing terms.

$16, 14\frac{1}{2}, \mathbf{13}, \mathbf{11\frac{1}{2}}, 10, \mathbf{8\frac{1}{2}}, 7, \mathbf{5\frac{1}{2}}$

You might have to use **reasoning** to show if a number would be a term in a sequence or not.

Example question: This sequence of numbers **decreases** by 30 each time.

3210, 3180, 3150, 3120 . . .

1220 will **not** be in the sequence. Explain how you know.

As well as decreasing by 30 each time, every term in this **arithmetic sequence** is a multiple of three. You can tell because the **digital sum** of each term is 3.

1220 is not a multiple of three so could not be in this sequence.

Encourage your child to measure the 'jumps' between each term when looking for how a sequence changes.

Parent tip!

Listen up 21

Pattern problems

Sometimes you have to work out a relationship or sequence to solve a problem.

Example question: Mrs Hodge is preparing the school canteen. She sets out the tables and chairs according to the pattern below. How many chairs will she need for 24 tables?

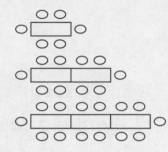

Number of Tables (t)	Number of Chairs (c)
1	6
2	10
3	14

Write an equation to show the relationship between the number of tables, t, and the number of chairs, c.

Look for a relationship between the number of tables and chairs.

If you multiply the number of tables by four and add two, you get the number of chairs.

So for 24 tables Mrs Hodge will need $(24 \times 4) + 2 = 98$ chairs.

The **equation** that describes the relationship between tables and chairs is

$$c = 4t + 2$$

Keywords

Linear number sequence ➤ A set of numbers that increases or decreases by the same amount each time

Common difference ➤ The amount that a linear number sequence increases or decreases by each time

Term ➤ A number in a sequence

Find out about some famous number sequences, for example the Fibonacci sequence or triangular numbers.

Have a go!

Test yourself

1 What is the next term in each sequence?

a. 32, 39, 46, 53, __

b. −12, −9, −6, −3, __

2 This number sequence increases by four each time. 12, 16, 20, 24, 28 … 248 will be in it. Explain why.

This mind map will help you remember all the main points from this topic. Have a go at drawing your own mind map.

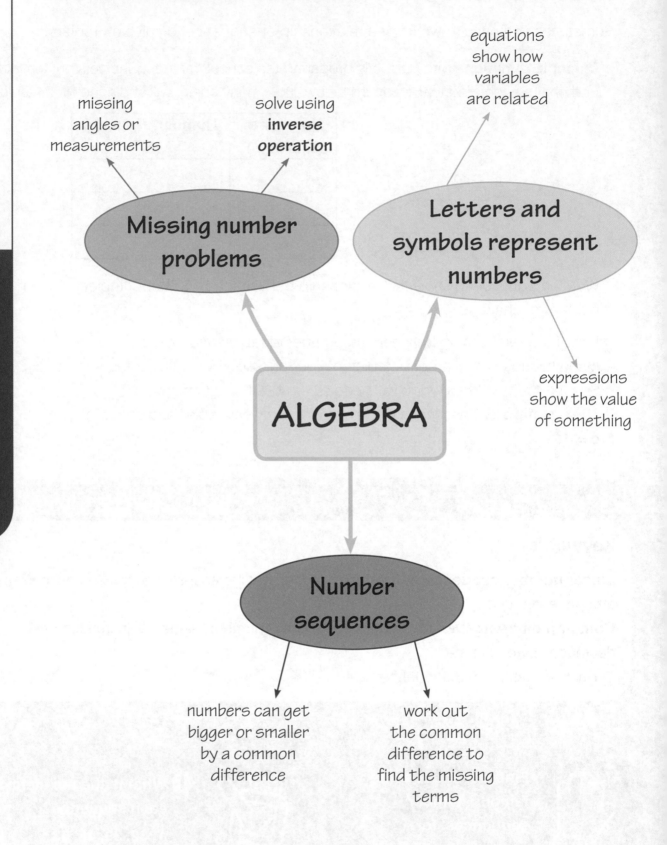

equations
show how
variables
are related

missing
angles or
measurements

solve using
**inverse
operation**

Missing number
problems

Letters and
symbols represent
numbers

ALGEBRA

expressions
show the value
of something

Number
sequences

numbers can get
bigger or smaller
by a common
difference

work out
the common
difference to
find the missing
terms

1 What are the missing numbers in these equations?

a. $50 - \boxed{} = 2 \times 18$ **(1 mark)** **b.** $84 \div 3 = \boxed{} \times 7$ **(1 mark)**

c. $\boxed{} + 12.5 = 3.7 + 9.3$ **(1 mark)**

2 What are the labelled angles in these triangles? **(2 marks)**

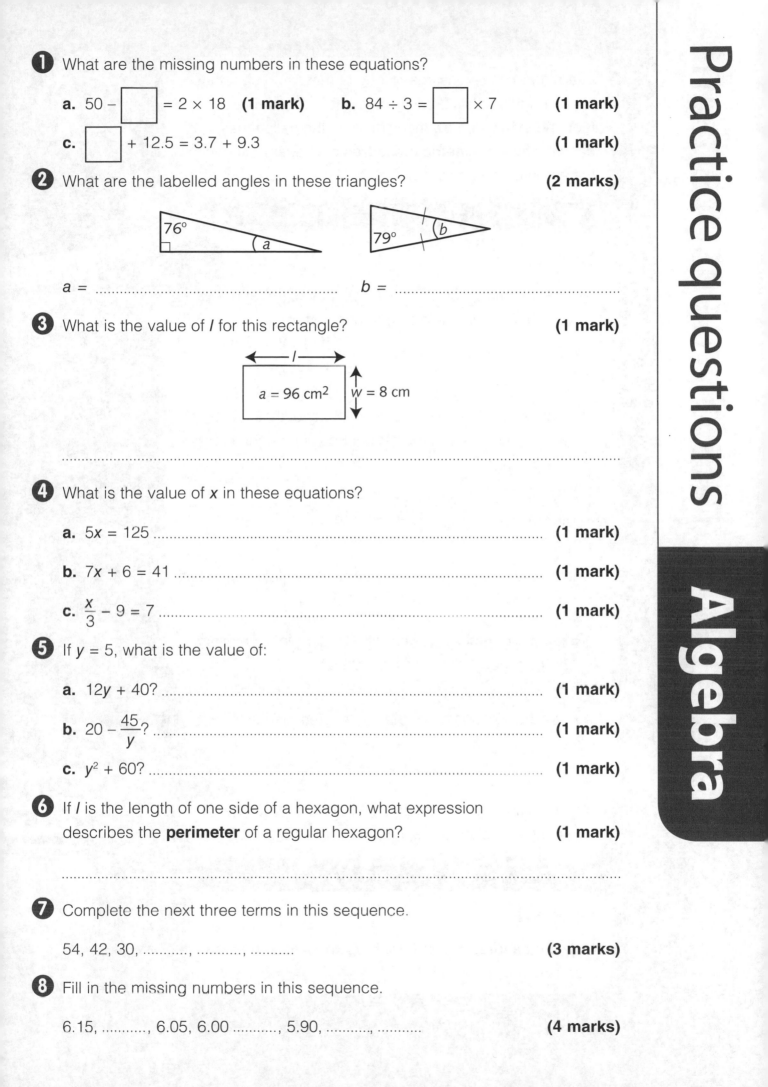

a = ... b = ...

3 What is the value of *l* for this rectangle? **(1 mark)**

....

4 What is the value of *x* in these equations?

a. $5x = 125$ .... **(1 mark)**

b. $7x + 6 = 41$ .... **(1 mark)**

c. $\frac{x}{3} - 9 = 7$ .... **(1 mark)**

5 If $y = 5$, what is the value of:

a. $12y + 40$? .... **(1 mark)**

b. $20 - \frac{45}{y}$? .... **(1 mark)**

c. $y^2 + 60$? .... **(1 mark)**

6 If *l* is the length of one side of a hexagon, what expression describes the **perimeter** of a regular hexagon? **(1 mark)**

....

7 Complete the next three terms in this sequence.

54, 42, 30, ..., ..., ... **(3 marks)**

8 Fill in the missing numbers in this sequence.

6.15, ..., 6.05, 6.00 ...., 5.90, ..., ... **(4 marks)**

Learning to use measures of length, mass and capacity is an important skill. Some grown-ups still talk about feet and inches or how many miles to the gallon their car will travel but **metric measures** are usually used in mathematics and science.

Length

Millimetres (mm), centimetres (cm), metres (m) and kilometres (km) are all related to each other.

×10   ×100   ×1000

1 mm   1 cm   1 m   1 km

1000 mm = 1 m
100 cm = 1 m
1000 m = 1 km

You can write a length or distance in any of these units of measurement or a combination. So your height might be written as:

- 1.35 m
- 135 cm
- 1 m 35 cm

> They are all the same.

When converting between units, move the digits to the left or right to make the number bigger or smaller.

Example question: Lee has fitted a garage door that is 2286 mm wide. What is this in metres?

One metre is 1000 mm.

To divide by 1000 move the digits three places to the right.

2286 mm ÷ 1000 = **2.286 m**

When multiplying or dividing by 10, 100 or 1000, the only thing that changes is the position of the digits.

Keyword

Metric measures ➤ A decimal system of measurement that uses multiples of 10

Mass and weight

Although they are different things, **mass** and **weight** both share the same metric units of measurement – grams (g) and kilograms (kg).

$$\times 1000$$
$$1\,\text{g} \quad\quad 1\,\text{kg}$$
$$1000\,\text{g} = 1\,\text{kg}$$

You can swap between these metric units by multiplying or dividing by 1000.

Example question: William has bought 0.198 kg of sweets. How many grams is this?

One kilogram is 1000 g.

To multiply by 1000 move the digits three places to the left.

$$0.198\,\text{kg} \times 1000 = 198\,\text{g}$$

Capacity

Capacity is usually measured in litres (l), millilitres (ml) and centilitres (cl).

$$\times 10 \quad\quad \times 100$$
$$1\,\text{ml} \quad\quad 1\,\text{cl} \quad\quad 1\,\text{l}$$
$$1000\,\text{ml} = 1\,\text{litre and } 100\,\text{cl} = 1\,\text{litre}$$

Example question: Sindri has bought a 33 cl soft drink. How many millilitres is this?

10 ml = 1 cl so multiply by 10.

Move the digits one place to the left and fill the ones place with a zero.

$$33\,\text{cl} \times 10 = 330\,\text{ml}$$

Keywords

Mass ➤ The amount of matter an object consists of. Your mass would be the same on Earth or in space

Weight ➤ The **mass** of an object multiplied by gravity

Capacity ➤ The amount of liquid that a container can hold

Top tip!

Learning what the prefixes **milli** (one thousandth), **centi** (one hundredth) and **kilo** (one thousand) mean will help you to convert between metric measures.

Have a go!

Find several drink or liquid containers. Arrange them in order from smallest to largest. Record their capacity in both millilitres and litres.

Test yourself

❶ Alfie is 147.2 cm tall and weighs 37.8 kg. Convert these measurements to metres and grams.

❷ Karol uses 160 g of sugar from a $\frac{1}{2}$ kg bag. How many grams are left?

Time is not measured in decimal units and can be represented in several ways. It can seem confusing! Learning to tell the time is one of the most important maths skills and one that you will use every day.

Units of measurement

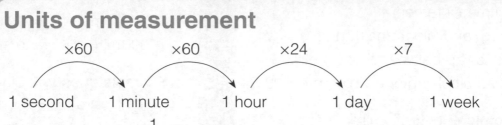

×60   ×60   ×24   ×7

1 second   1 minute   1 hour   1 day   1 week

The Earth takes $365\frac{1}{4}$ days to orbit the Sun, so every fourth or **leap year** has 366 days. The twelve months of the year also have a varying number of days:

"Thirty days have September,
April, June, and November.
All the rest have 31,
Except February alone,
And that has 28 days clear,
And 29 in a leap year."

Analogue and digital clocks

Clocks are either **digital** or **analogue**. Time before midday is am, after midday it becomes pm.

Most **digital** clocks can be set to show the time as either 12 or 24 hours. Twenty-four hour times are the same until midday. Then add 12 hours to the pm time. So 2.30pm is 14.30.

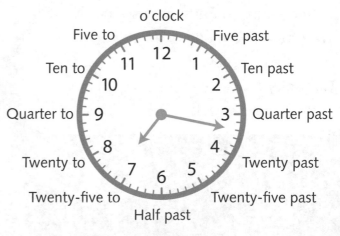

Always use four digits for 24 hour times, for example 7.20am would be 07.20.

You will have learned to read the time on an **analogue** clock. As well as o'clock, half past, quarter past and quarter to, you should know all the minutes past and minutes to.

Elapsed time problems

If you know when an event starts and ends, you can work out the difference between the two times.

Use a time line and write down the intervals between the two times. Then add the intervals up to find out how much time has passed.

Example: A train leaves London at 08.45 and arrives in Edinburgh at 14.19. How long is the journey?

Draw a time line with the departure and arrival times on it.

08.45   14.19

Decide on some intervals that you can 'hop' between.
O'clock times are usually the best.

15 mins   5 hrs   19 mins

08:45 09:00   14:00 14:19

Add the 'hops' to find the total journey time.
15 mins + 5 hrs + 19 mins = 5 hrs 34 mins

Keywords

Digital ➤ A clock that shows the hour followed by the number of minutes past the hour, usually separated by a colon

Analogue ➤ A clock with a circular face, usually marked with the numerals 1–12 and an hour and a minute hand

Parent tip!
An inexpensive wrist watch, preferably analogue rather than digital, is a great way to get children talking about and using time from an early age.

Have a go!
Collect a train, ferry, tram or bus timetable. Use it to work out the lengths of five different journeys.

Test yourself

1 a. How many seconds are in two hours?

   b. How many hours are in a week?

2 Write these as 24 hour digital times.

   a. 5.48pm

   b. Quarter to one in the morning

3 Alison's Metro train from Whitley Bay to West Jesmond departs at 13.52 and arrives at 14.19. How long is her journey?

There are many countries including the UK that use **imperial measures**. You can buy pints of milk and some people talk about their height in feet and inches. You need to be able to convert between some of these and their metric equivalents.

Top tip!

When converting between metric and imperial measures, remember which unit is larger. For example, when changing miles to kilometres, you know that your answer will be larger because a mile is longer than a kilometre.

Length

A 30 cm ruler is **approximately** one foot long. It might be marked in inches on one side and centimetres on the other.

You can show **approximations** using a **symbol**.

One foot is approximately 30 cm.   1 foot ≈ 30 cm

One inch is approximately $2\frac{1}{2}$ cm.   1 inch ≈ 2.5 cm

You can use these facts to make approximate conversions.

> **Example question**: A frog is 4 inches long. Approximately how long is this in centimetres?
>
> One inch is approximately 2.5 cm so multiply 4 by 2.5
>
> $4 \times 2.5\,cm = 10\,cm$
>
> So the frog is approximately 10 cm long.

Longer distances are often measured in miles.

One mile is approximately 1.6 km.   1 mile ≈ 1.6 km

Multiplying by 1.6 will convert a distance in miles to one in kilometres.

But what if you had to convert from kilometres to miles? It is harder to divide by 1.6.

A kilometre is approximately 0.6, $\frac{6}{10}$ or 60 percent of a mile, so you can multiply by 0.6.

Keywords

Imperial measures ➤ Units of measurement that used to be common in the UK. Some are still used today

Approximately ➤ An answer or equation that is not completely accurate but close enough to be useful. The symbol ≈ may be used to show this

listen up 24

Conversion graphs

A **conversion graph** makes it easier to switch between miles and kilometres.

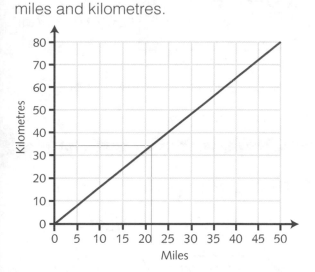

Example question: Use the conversion graph to convert 35 kilometres to miles.

Use a ruler to draw a **horizontal** line across from 35 km until it meets the conversion line. Draw a line vertically down from the conversion line to the *x* axis. Now you can read the distance in miles. It's close to 21. So 35 km ≈ 21 miles.

The graph works both ways. You can use it to convert miles to kilometres.

Other imperial measures

Adults might refer to their weight in stones (st) and pounds (lb). A pound is **approximately** 450 g. A stone is 14 lb.

1 lb ~ 450 g

When baking you might see ounces (oz) in a recipe. An ounce is **approximately** 25 g. A pound is 16 oz.

1 oz ≈ 25 g

The milkman delivers pints of milk. Drivers discuss how many miles to the gallon of fuel their cars will travel. One pint is **approximately** 570 ml. A gallon is 8 pints.

1 pt ≈ 570 ml

Keyword

Conversion graph ➤
A line graph that shows the relationship between two different units of measurement

Measure your own height and weight in metric units. Convert them to imperial ones. If they let you, do the same for friends or other members of your family.

Have a go!

Test yourself

① **Aniyah is 3 feet and 10 inches tall. Approximately how many centimetres is this?**

② **Use the conversion graph to estimate how many kilometres are equivalent to:**

a. **12 miles**   b. **26 miles**

c. **44 miles**

Area of a rectangle

You can calculate the **area** of any rectangle by multiplying the length (l) by the width (w).

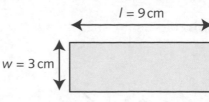

$l = 9\,cm$

$w = 3\,cm$

$9\,cm \times 3\,cm = 27\,cm^2$

Include the units of measurement, in this case square centimetres or cm^2.

The relationship between length (l), width (w) and area (a) as a formula is: $a = lw$

Area of parallelograms and triangles

There are **formulae** you can use to find the area of these **polygons**.

To find the area (a) of a **parallelogram** multiply the base (b) by the height (h).

$a = bh$

$h = 4\,cm$

$b = 7\,cm$

$7\,cm \times 4\,cm = 28\,cm^2$

You can see how this works if you drag one of the right-angled triangle 'ends' of the parallelogram across.

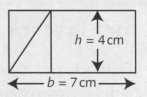

$h = 4\,cm$

$b = 7\,cm$

It makes a rectangle with a length (or base) of 7 cm and width (or height) of 4 cm.

For the area (a) of **triangles** you need to multiply the base (b) by the height (h) and then halve the result.

$a = \dfrac{bh}{2}$

$h = 5\,cm$

$b = 8\,cm$

$\dfrac{5\,cm \times 8\,cm}{2} = \dfrac{40\,cm^2}{2} = 20\,cm^2$

You can see why this works in right-angled triangles. These are clearly half of a rectangle.

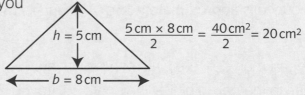

$h = 5\,cm$

$b = 8\,cm$

$\dfrac{5\,cm \times 8\,cm}{2} = \dfrac{40\,cm^2}{2} = 20\,cm^2$

Keywords

Area ➤ The size that a surface takes up measured in 'square' **units of measurement**, e.g. square metres (m^2)

Polygon ➤ Any 2D shape with three or more straight sides

Perimeter

You can find the **perimeter** by measuring the distance around the edges.

The **perimeter** of a rectangle is double the length + width. The formula is: $p = 2(l + w)$

Example question: A tennis court is 23.78 m long and 10.97 m wide. What is the **perimeter**?

The perimeter will be double 23.78 m + 10.97 m.

$2 \times (23.78\,m + 10.97\,m)$

$2 \times 34.75\,m = \textbf{69.5 m}$

Top tip!

To find the perimeter of any **regular polygon** multiply the length of one side by the number of sides.

Keyword

Perimeter ➤ The distance around the outside of a shape. The perimeter of a circle is called the **circumference**

Have a go!

On some centimetre squared paper see how many different rectangles you can draw with an area of 24 cm². Although they all have the same area, do they all have the same perimeter?

Test yourself

① A rectangle that is 12 cm long has an area of 60 cm². How wide is it?

② What are the areas of these shapes?

8 cm

14 cm

10 cm

20 cm

③ A netball court is 30.5 m long and 15.25 m wide. What is its perimeter?

Volume is a measure of how much space is taken up by any three dimensional (3D) object. It might describe a liquid, a gas or a solid.

Calculating volume

You may have built 3D shapes out of centimetre cubes. The volume of the shape is equivalent to the number of cubes it is built out of.

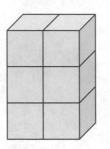

This cuboid is made up of six centimetre cubes. It has a volume of 6 cubic centimetres, 6 centimetres cubed or $6\,cm^3$.

To calculate the volume (v) of a cuboid, multiply the length (l) by the width (w) by the height (h).

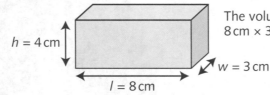

$h = 4\,cm$

$l = 8\,cm$

$w = 3\,cm$

The volume is $8\,cm \times 3\,cm \times 4\,cm$
$8\,cm \times 3\,cm \times 4\,cm = 96\,cm^3$

This can be written as a **formula**:

$v = lwh$

Example question: Neptune's World is planning to build a new aquarium to hold their shark collection. It will be 25 m long, 10 m wide and 6 m deep. How many cubic metres of sea water will be needed to fill it?

To find the volume, multiply the three dimensions of the new aquarium together.

$$25\,m \times 10\,m \times 6\,m = \mathbf{1500\,m^3}$$

Solving problems

Sometimes you might know the volume but one of the dimensions might be missing.

Example question: Rhian has built a cuboid using 72 centimetre cubes. Her cuboid is 6 cm long and 4 cm wide. How high is it?

Use the formula for the volume of a cuboid, $v = lwh$.

$72 = 6 \times 4 \times \boxed{}$ $72 = 24 \times \boxed{}$

Use the **inverse** operation to find the missing height.

$$72 \div 24 = 3$$

So the height of Rhian's cuboid is 3 cm.

Listen up 26

Imagine a measuring jug with some milk in. The jug has a **capacity** of 750 ml but the **volume** of milk in the jug might be less, for example 200 ml.

Top tip!

Keyword

Volume ➤ The amount of space taken up by a three dimensional (3D) object, measured in cubic units, e.g. cubic centimetres (cm³)

Have a go!

Choose five cuboid food boxes from your kitchen cupboards.

Estimate their volumes and arrange them in order from smallest to biggest.

Use a ruler to measure and then calculate their volumes in cubic centimetres. How close were your estimates?

Test yourself

1. A cardboard box is 35 cm long, 15 cm wide and 20 cm high. What is its volume in cubic centimetres?

2. A dairy farmer has a tank that has a square base measuring 2 m on each side. She fills it to a depth of 1.25 m with milk. What is the volume of milk in the tank?

3. The owners of a zoo want to build an aviary with a volume of 400 cubic metres. What could the dimensions of the aviary be?

This mind map will help you remember all the main points from this topic. Have a go at drawing your own mind map.

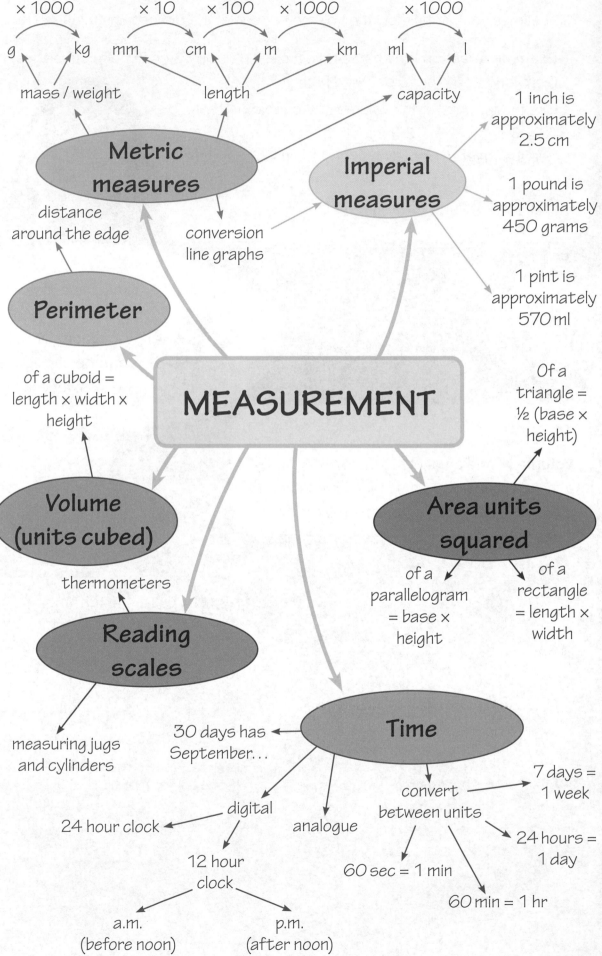

× 1000

× 10   × 100   × 1000

× 1000

g ⟷ kg   mm cm m km   ml ⟷ l

mass / weight   length   capacity

Metric measures

Imperial measures

1 inch is approximately 2.5 cm

1 pound is approximately 450 grams

1 pint is approximately 570 ml

distance around the edge

conversion line graphs

Perimeter

MEASUREMENT

of a cuboid = length × width × height

Of a triangle = ½ (base × height)

Volume (units cubed)

Area units squared

thermometers

of a parallelogram = base × height

of a rectangle = length × width

Reading scales

measuring jugs and cylinders

30 days has September…

Time

7 days = 1 week

digital

convert between units

24 hour clock

analogue

24 hours = 1 day

12 hour clock

60 sec = 1 min

60 min = 1 hr

a.m. (before noon)

p.m. (after noon)

1 Convert these lengths to centimetres.

 a. 9.05 m .... **(1 mark)** **b.** $4\frac{1}{2}$ m .... **(1 mark)**

2 Convert these weights to grams.

 a. $25\frac{3}{4}$ kg .... **(1 mark)** **b.** 8.067 kg .... **(1 mark)**

3 Write these 24 hr times as 12 hr digital times and show if they are am or pm.

 a. 16.48 .... **(1 mark)** **b.** 00.30 .... **(1 mark)**

4 a. Tiana runs a race in 6 minutes and 34 seconds.

 How many seconds is this? .... **(1 mark)**

 b. Karol's flight lasts 4 and three-quarters hours.

 How many minutes is this? .... **(1 mark)**

5 The coach from Norwich to Liverpool leaves at 03.05 and arrives at 15.40. How long is the journey? **(1 mark)**

....

6 This line graph helps convert temperatures between degrees Centigrade and Fahrenheit.

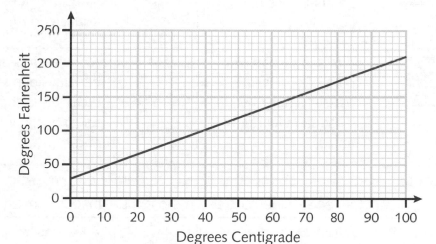

Approximately how many °F are:

a. 50°C .... **(1 mark)** **b.** 15°C .... **(1 mark)**

Approximately how many °C are:

c. 200°F .... **(1 mark)** **d.** 80°F .... **(1 mark)**

7 Martha wants to know the volume of a parcel before she goes to post it. It is 35 cm long, 15 cm wide and 10 cm high.

What is the volume of the parcel in cubic centimetres? **(1 mark)**

....

Geometry

2D shapes have two dimensions. These are length and width.

3D or three dimensional shapes have length, width and height.

2D shapes

Polygons are classified according to their properties, for example how many sides they have.

Example question: What are the properties of this pentagon?

It has five straight sides.

It is **regular** because all sides and angles are equal.

It has five **diagonals**, straight lines joining non-adjacent corners.

Polygons with four sides are called **quadrilaterals**. There are six that you need to describe.

	A parallelogram has two pairs of opposite **parallel** sides of equal length.		A rhombus has opposite parallel sides. All sides are of equal length.
	A rectangle has two pairs of opposite parallel sides of equal length and four right angles.		A square has opposite parallel sides. All sides are of equal length and it has four right angles.

It can get confusing! All of these shapes qualify as parallelograms. And a square is a rectangle with four equal sides but also a rhombus with four right angles!

	A trapezium has only one pair of opposite parallel sides.		A kite has two pairs of **adjacent** sides that are equal in length.

Polygons with three sides are called **triangles**. There are four that you need to know.

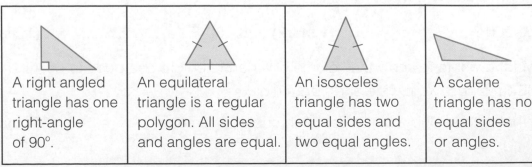

A right angled triangle has one right-angle of 90°.	An equilateral triangle is a regular polygon. All sides and angles are equal.	An isosceles triangle has two equal sides and two equal angles.	A scalene triangle has no equal sides or angles.

3D shapes

You can describe any **polyhedron** (a 3D shape with flat faces) by how many **faces**, **edges** and **vertices** it has.

Surfaces meet at an **edge**

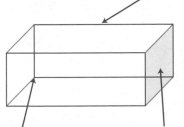

Edges meet at a **vertex**

Each surface is a **face**

If you count them you can see that the **cuboid** above has 6 faces, 12 edges and 8 vertices.

You can get the **net** of a shape by unfolding it and laying it out flat.

Example question:

Which of these two nets would fold up to make a cube?

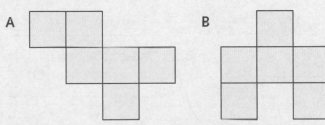

A   B

Leave one of the centre faces as a base. Fold the other faces up to create the cube. Only **net A** will work.

Keywords

Polygon ➤ A 2D shape with straight sides
Polyhedron ➤ A 3D shape with flat faces
Regular ➤ A polygon that has all sides and all angles equal
Diagonal ➤ A straight line that joins non-adjacent corners of a polygon
Parallel ➤ Lines that always stay the same distance apart and never meet
Adjacent ➤ Corners or sides that are next to each other are adjacent

Top tip!

The angles in polygons add up to totals that are always the same, e.g. in a triangle it is always 180°, in quadrilaterals the total is 360°. You can use this to find missing angles.

Listen up 27

Have a go!

There is a *formula* that describes the relationship between the numbers of faces, edges and vertices in a polyhedron. Try to discover what it is.

Test yourself

① What is the name of any eight-sided polygon?

② Why is a rhombus not a regular polygon?

③ What are the other two angles in a right-angled triangle that is also an isosceles triangle?

④ How many faces, edges and vertices are there in a pentagonal prism?

⑤ Draw the net of a triangular prism.

An **angle** measures the amount of turn around a point in degrees. There are 360° in a full circle.

Circles and turns

The **diameter** (*d*) is the distance through the centre of the circle. It connects two points on the **circumference**.

The **circumference** (*c*) is the distance all the way around the outside of the circle.

The **radius** (*r*) is the distance from the centre of the circle to any point on the **circumference**.

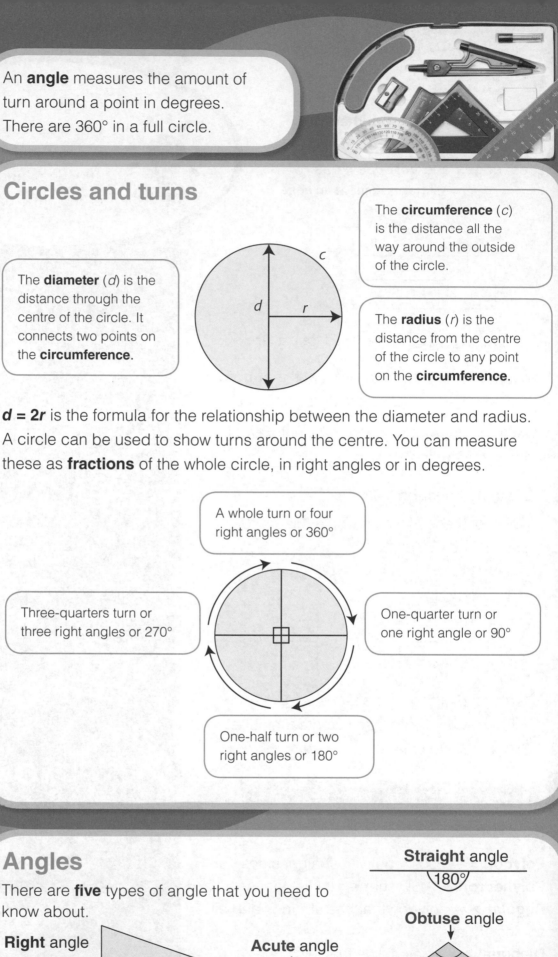

d = 2r is the formula for the relationship between the diameter and radius. A circle can be used to show turns around the centre. You can measure these as **fractions** of the whole circle, in right angles or in degrees.

A whole turn or four right angles or 360°

Three-quarters turn or three right angles or 270°

One-quarter turn or one right angle or 90°

One-half turn or two right angles or 180°

Angles

There are **five** types of angle that you need to know about.

Right angle or 90°

Acute angle

Straight angle 180°

Obtuse angle

Reflex angle

Listen up 28

Missing angles

Remember these three angle facts to calculate a missing angle.

- Angles on a straight line total 180°.

Example question: Calculate angle *b*.

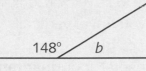

148°   *b*

$148° + b = 180°$
So $180° - 148 = b$

b = **32°**

- Angles that meet at a point total 360°.

Example question: Calculate angle *c*.

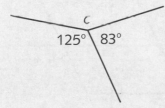

c
125°   83°

$125° + 83° + c = 360°$
$208° + c = 360°$
So $360° - 208° = c$

c = **152°**

- When lines cross, the opposite angles are equal.

Example question: Calculate angle *d*.

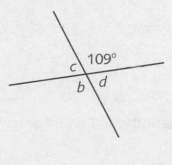

c 109°
b   *d*

Opposite angles are equal,
so angle *b* will be 109°.
Double 109° = 218°.

Remember that angles around a point total 360°.
$360° - 218° = 142°$
Because *c* and *d* are also equal you know that
142° is the value of *c* and *d* added together.
$142° \div 2 = 71°$

d = **71°**

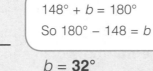
Keywords

Acute ➤ Any angle less than 90°

Obtuse ➤ Any angle between 90° and 180°

Reflex ➤ Any angle between 180° and 360°

Straight angle ➤ An angle that is exactly 180°

Have a go!

Angles in a triangle add up to 180° and angles in a quadrilateral add up to 360°.

Draw some other polygons and see what the totals for these shapes are.
Use your protractor.

Test yourself

❶ The diameter of a circle is 25 cm. What is its radius?

❷ How many degrees in one and a quarter turns?

❸ Why can't a triangle have two obtuse angles?

You can describe where a point is located using its **coordinates**. Several points can be joined to create **polygons** that can be **translated** or **reflected**.

Coordinates

In coordinates, the first number is the distance you have to travel horizontally along the *x* axis. The second number is the distance you travel vertically along the *y* axis. Both axes begin at (0, 0). This is the **origin**.
If you know how to use **negative numbers**, you can use all four **quadrants**.

Example question: What are the coordinates of the corners of the parallelogram ABCD?

This parallelogram has a corner in each **quadrant**. Start at the **origin** for each one.

A is straightforward. Count three along the *x* axis and climb two along the *y* axis to find **(3, 2)**.

For **B** count along the *x* axis but go down the *y* axis. This gives it a negative value, **(1, –2)**.

C has both a negative *x* and *y* value. You have to move backwards along the *x* axis and down the *y* axis to get **(–3, –2)**.

To find **D** travel back along the *x* axis before climbing up the *y* axis to arrive at **(–1, 2)**.

Sometimes the axes will not be numbered. Use **reasoning** to find missing coordinates.

Example question: Here is a square on a coordinate axis. What are the coordinates of C and D?

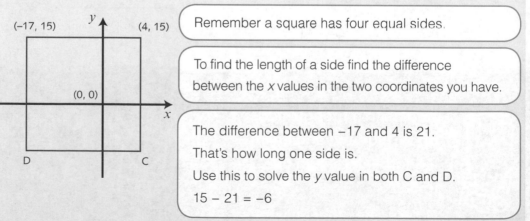

Remember a square has four equal sides.

To find the length of a side find the difference between the *x* values in the two coordinates you have.

The difference between –17 and 4 is 21. That's how long one side is.
Use this to solve the *y* value in both C and D.
15 – 21 = –6

So C is **(4, –6)** and D is **(–17, –6)**.

Reflections and translations

You can move a polygon to a new position on a grid through **translation** and **reflection**.

You can show a translation by using an **expression**. You can also change the position of a shape by **reflection** in a mirror line, which might be the x or y axis or any other straight line.

Example question 1: Triangle ABC is translated so that $(x, y) \rightarrow (x + 2, y - 4)$. Draw the new position of the triangle on the grid.

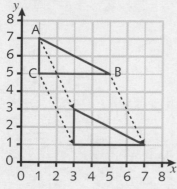

All the corners of the triangle move the same amount. So add two to every x value and subtract four from every y value.

Corner	Coordinate	New Coordinate
A	(1, 7)	(3, 3)
B	(5, 5)	(7, 1)
C	(1, 5)	(3, 1)

Example question 2: Reflect the trapezium ABCD in the y axis.

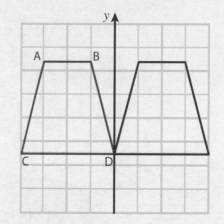

Measure the distance of each point from the mirror line (in this case the y axis). Continue for the same distance on the other side of the mirror line.

Draw a dot and join these together to find the new position of the new 'flipped' shape.

Keywords

Coordinates ➤ Pairs of numbers that show the exact position of a point on a grid

Translation ➤ Move or 'slide' a shape to a new position on a grid without changing its size or appearance

Reflection ➤ A shape 'flipped' across a mirror line without changing its size

Quadrant ➤ Four areas created when a grid is divided with an x and a y axis

Have a go! Draw a 6 × 6 grid. Take turns to plot coordinates by rolling two dice, one for the x value and one for the y value. The winner is the first player to plot three points in a line (vertically, diagonally or horizontally).

Test yourself

❶ What is a translation?

❷ What is the second number in a coordinate?

Geometry

This mind map will help you remember all the main points from this topic. Have a go at drawing your own mind map.

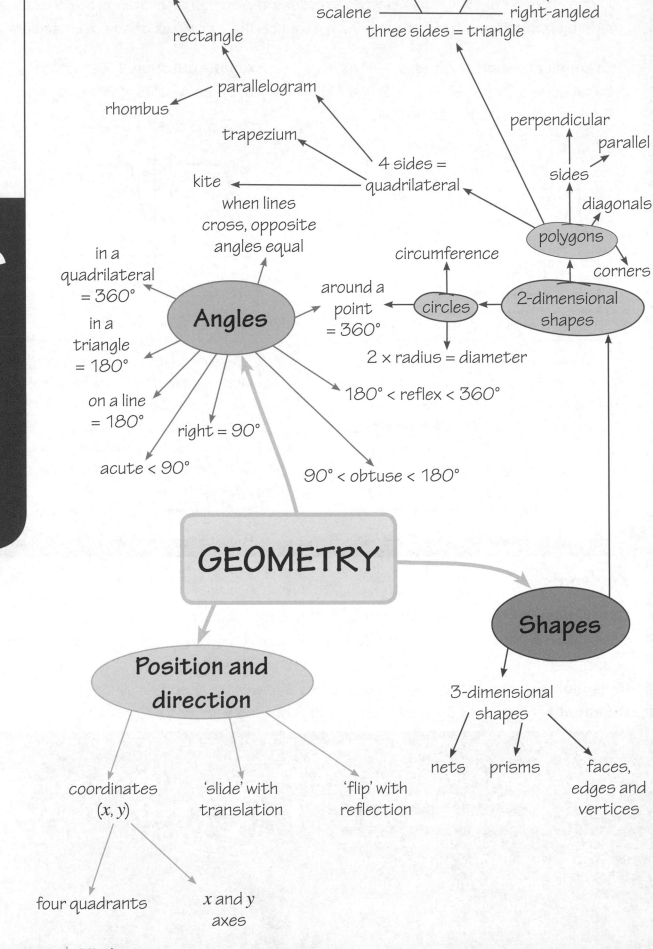

❶ Tammy says that her isosceles triangle has angles of 45°, 35° and 100°. Explain why she is wrong. **(1 mark)**

....

❷ Calculate the missing angles in these diagrams. **(3 marks)**

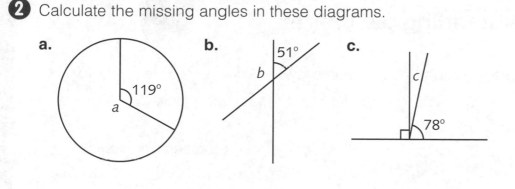

a.   b.   c.

....

❸ This diagram shows a rectangle on a coordinate grid. What are the coordinates of points B and D? **(2 marks)**

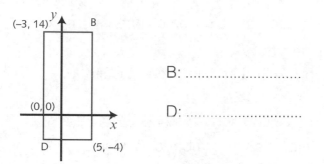

B: ....

D: ....

❹ **a.** Write the coordinates of each corner of the pentagon ABCDE. **(1 mark)**

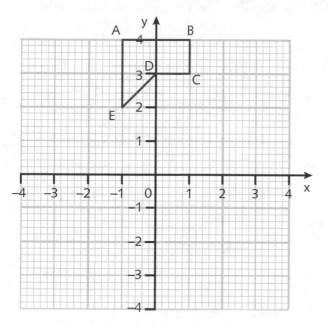

A: ....

B: ....

C: ....

D: ....

E: ....

b. Translate the pentagon ABCDE so that $(x, y) \rightarrow (x - 2, y - 5)$. Draw the new position. **(1 mark)**

c. Reflect the original pentagon ABCDE in the *x*–axis and draw the new position. **(1 mark)**

Understanding pie charts

Example question: This pie chart shows favourite football teams in Year 6. There are 28 children in the class and nine support United. How many support City?

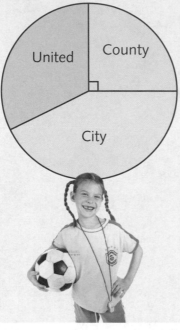

All 28 children are represented by **slices** or sectors of the pie chart.

The sector for City is the biggest. They have most supporters. But how many?

The right angle tells you that the County sector represents a quarter of the children. $\frac{1}{4}$ of 28 = 7, so seven children support County.

You know that nine support United.

7 + 9 = 16

The United and County sectors total 16. Calculate the number of City supporters.

28 − 16 = 12

Sometimes you need to use what you know about percentages to make sense of a pie chart.

Example question: This pie chart shows where the children at Wellington Lane Primary live. What percentage of children live in terraced houses?

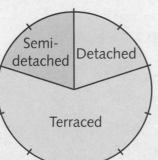

The pie chart has been split into 10 equal sections.

Children who live in terraced houses take up six of these tenths.

One tenth is 10 percent so six tenths would be 60 percent.

60 percent of the children live in terraced houses.

Drawing pie charts

Pie charts show amounts from 360 because there are 360 degrees in a circle.

Imagine that you have collected some data on favourite pets.

Display it as a pie chart.

Dogs	Cats	Others	Total
8	5	7	20

The total of 20 pets will occupy all 360° of the circle.

So one pet would be worth 360° ÷ 20 = 18°.

Multiply each pet by this amount.

Dogs	Cats	Others	Total
8	5	7	20
8 × 18° = 144°	5 × 18° = 90°	7 × 18° = 126°	360°

Parent tip!

Look at how tables, graphs and charts (not just pie charts) are used to make information easier to understand. Find examples on TV, in newspapers or on websites and talk about what they show.

You have the angle for each sector in your pie chart.

Use an angle measurer or protractor to draw your pie chart.

Create a circle using a pair of compasses or draw around your protractor.

Keywords

Pie chart ➤ A chart that shows the relative sizes of data as sectors of a circle

Data ➤ A collection of information which might be numbers, facts or measurements. Data is often organised into tables and displayed as charts or graphs to make it easier to understand

Have a go!

Collect some data of your own.

It could be your favourite teams or makes of car that you identify in a survey.

Once you have your data, write it into a table and display it as a pie chart. You will need a protractor and something circular to draw around.

Test yourself

This pie chart shows bed times for the 32 children in Class 6.

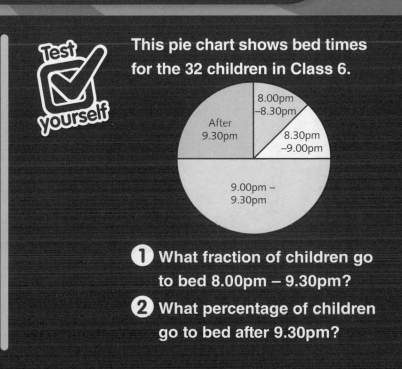

❶ What fraction of children go to bed 8.00pm – 9.30pm?

❷ What percentage of children go to bed after 9.30pm?

Line graphs

Line graphs show how one thing varies in comparison with another. **Averages** help you make sense of data that isn't displayed in a table or as a chart or a graph.

Many line graphs show how something changes over time. If the data is **continuous**, you can use the graph to make predictions.

> **Top tip!** When drawing your own line graphs, use a ruler and a sharp pencil. Check the maximum value for each axis. Divide each axis up into equal steps, e.g. every 10, 20 or 50 units. Remember to label each axis and give a unit of measurement.

Example question: Joe measured the length of a shadow five times over the day. He plotted his measurements on this line graph.

a. Joe predicts that at 07.00 the shadow would have been between 130 cm and 140 cm long. Is he right?

b. At what two times during the day would the shadow have been a metre long?

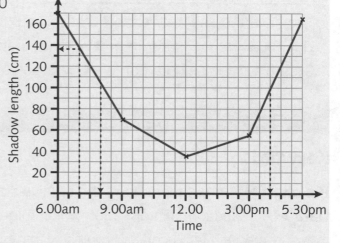

Part a. – draw a vertical line up from 7.00am until it meets the line. Read across to the vertical axis to find the length of shadow at this time. It's **approximately** 135 cm so Joe's prediction is correct.

Part b. – read the graph the other way. Use a ruler to travel horizontally across from 100 cm to find two places where you cross the line. Read vertically down to read the horizontal axis at **approximately** 8.00am and 4.00pm.

Line graphs can be used to convert between different units of measurement, for example miles and kilometres.

Listen up **31**

Keyword

Continuous data ➤ Can have any value within a certain range, e.g. the temperature throughout the day

Averages

Imagine you measured the height of all the children in your class. How does your height compare to that of your classmates? Calculating the **average** or **mean** value helps you to answer this.

Example question: Bilal receives £3.60 a week pocket money. His five friends receive £4.00, £2.50, £2.50, £5.00 and £3.10. Does Bilal receive below or above average pocket money?

£3.60 + £4.00 + £2.50 + £2.50 + £5.00 + £3.10 = £20.70 ← Firstly add up all of the values. Include Bilal's pocket money as well!

£20.70 ÷ 6 = £3.45 ← Then, divide the total by the number of values to find the **mean**.

So Bilal receives a little above the average amount.

Keyword

Mean ➤ The total of all the values divided by the number of values. Also called the **arithmetic average**

Have a go!

Have you got some old coins in your house from a foreign holiday?

Find out the current exchange rate for that currency. Draw a conversion graph up to £100.

Test yourself

This graph will help you convert between British pounds and Polish zlotys.

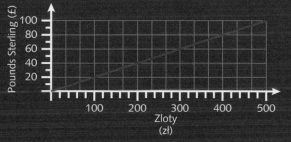

1 Approximately how many zlotys are there for:

    a. £40   b. £80   c. £25

2 Approximately how many pounds are there for:

    a. 300 zł   b. 80 zł   c. 380 zł

This mind map will help you remember all the main points from this topic. Have a go at drawing your own mind map.

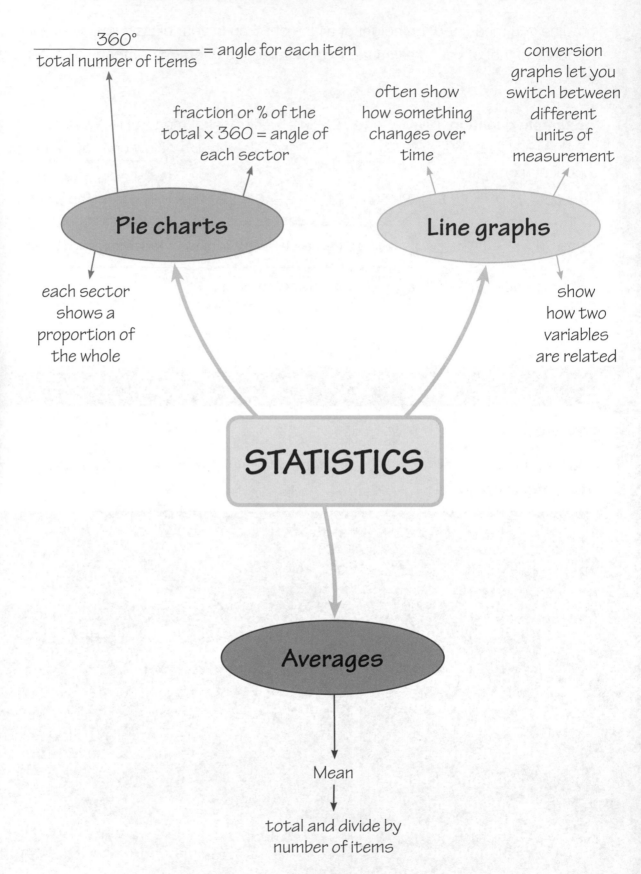

$$\frac{360°}{\text{total number of items}} = \text{angle for each item}$$

fraction or % of the total × 360 = angle of each sector

Pie charts

each sector shows a proportion of the whole

often show how something changes over time

conversion graphs let you switch between different units of measurement

Line graphs

show how two variables are related

STATISTICS

Averages

Mean

total and divide by number of items

1 Children took part in a trial for a new breakfast cereal.
This pie chart shows which cereal they liked best.

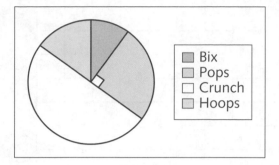

- Bix
- Pops
- Crunch
- Hoops

The most popular cereal was chosen by 270 children.

95 children chose 'Hoops'.

Place a ✓ or a ✗ in each box to show if the statement is correct.

a. 540 children took part in the trial. ☐   **(1 mark)**

b. One-quarter preferred 'Pops'. ☐   **(1 mark)**

c. One-fifth preferred 'Hoops'. ☐   **(1 mark)**

d. 10 percent preferred 'Bix'. ☐   **(1 mark)**

2 In a test, seven children scored 24, 24, 37, 38, 40, 39 and 43.
What was the average (mean) score?   **(1 mark)**

3 A scientist records the temperature in this table at six times over
a 24-hour period.

00:00	04:00	08:00	12:00	16:00	20:00
–2°C	–3°C	3°C	7°C	8°C	5°C

What is the average (mean) temperature?

.... **(1 mark)**

4 Four children ran 100 m. Three of the children ran it in 22 s, 18 s and 19 s.
The average (mean) time was 20 s.

What was the fourth child's time?

.... **(1 mark)**

Practice questions

Statistics

SATs Practice Questions

1. 427 + 384 =

1 mark

2. 627 – 153 =

1 mark

3. Show your method

		2	2	3	6
	×			3	7

2 marks

4. Show your method

$$12\overline{)3792}$$

2 marks

5 0.73 + 15.2195 =

1 mark

6 $3^2 + \boxed{} = 68$

1 mark

7 $18 \times 4 = 12 \times \boxed{}$

1 mark

8 $3\frac{2}{5} + 2\frac{1}{4} =$

1 mark

9 Use these number cards in this equation to make it correct. 7 4 3 4 **(1 mark)**

$$1\,\frac{\square}{\square} = \frac{\square}{\square}$$

10 This is a plan of a garden.

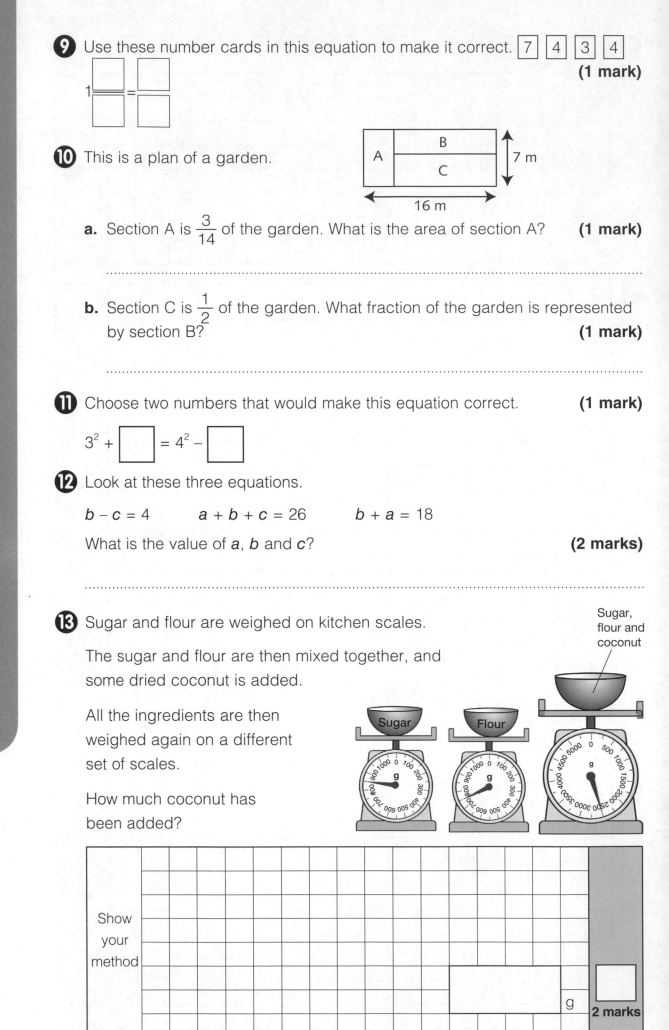

A | B | C | 7 m | 16 m

a. Section A is $\frac{3}{14}$ of the garden. What is the area of section A? **(1 mark)**

....

b. Section C is $\frac{1}{2}$ of the garden. What fraction of the garden is represented by section B? **(1 mark)**

....

11 Choose two numbers that would make this equation correct. **(1 mark)**

$$3^2 + \boxed{} = 4^2 - \boxed{}$$

12 Look at these three equations.

$b - c = 4$ $\qquad$ $a + b + c = 26$ $\qquad$ $b + a = 18$

What is the value of *a*, *b* and *c*? **(2 marks)**

....

13 Sugar and flour are weighed on kitchen scales.

The sugar and flour are then mixed together, and some dried coconut is added.

All the ingredients are then weighed again on a different set of scales.

How much coconut has been added?

Sugar, flour and coconut

Sugar | Flour

Show your method

g

2 marks

14 Rosie is buying a phone.

In Smartech it cost £145, but is now 15 percent cheaper.

At Fastfone it cost £160, but she can save $\frac{1}{5}$ of the original price.

Rosie says, "It's cheaper from Fastfone."

Is she right? Circle Yes / No

Show how you know. **(2 marks)**

....

....

....

15 Here is an equilateral triangle and a square.

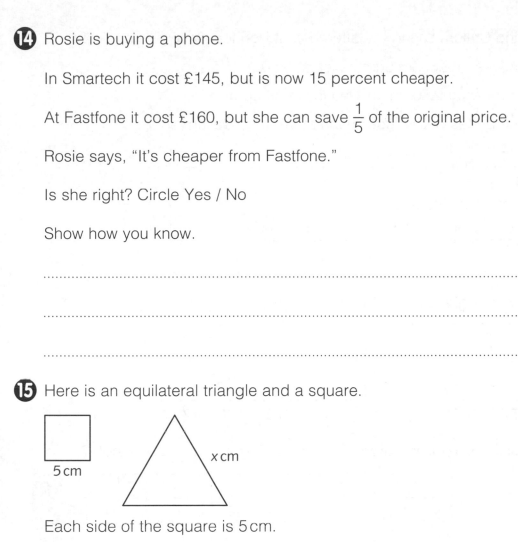

5 cm

x cm

Each side of the square is 5 cm.

Each side of the triangle is x cm.

The perimeter of six squares is equal to the perimeter of four triangles.

What number is represented by x? **(1 mark)**

....

....

16 **a.** Miss Smith has y tables in the classroom. Three more are delivered.

What expression describes the number of tables in
the classroom now? **(1 mark)**

....

b. Chen has five tables each with x chairs. He stacks the chairs up then
removes six. What expression describes the number of chairs in the
stack now? **(1 mark)**

....

17 Ethan and Callum spend the afternoon at Bounce Nation trampolining.

Ethan arrives at 2.30pm and leaves at 3.50pm.

Callum arrives at 2.50pm and leaves at 4.20pm.

Using the prices below, how much more does Callum spend than Ethan?

(1 mark)

Prices:
£4.00 for up to an hour.
Then, £1.00 for every 10 minutes after this.

18 Here is a triangle and a parallelogram.

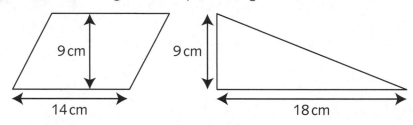

9 cm   14 cm   9 cm   18 cm

How much bigger is the area of the parallelogram than the triangle?

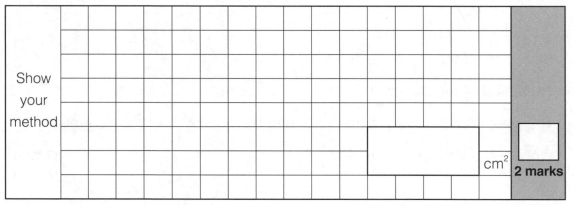

Show your method

cm²

2 marks

19 Calculate the value of angle **z**.

(1 mark)

43°

z

20 Triangle ABC is isosceles. Calculate the value of angle *y*.

(1 mark)

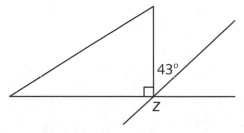

24°

y   y

21 An aquarium is 60 cm long by 50 cm wide by 60 cm high.

Mick is filling the tank with water using a bottle with a capacity of 6000 cubic centimetres. How many bottles will he need to pour into the tank to fill it?

Show your method

2 marks

22 Look at the rectangle on the grid below.

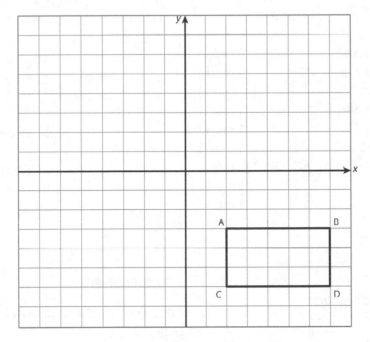

This rectangle ABCD has been translated so that $(x, y) \rightarrow (x - 1, y - 8)$ and then reflected in the **y** axis. On the grid above, draw the position of the rectangle **before** both of these transformations.   **(1 mark)**

23 This pie chart shows which school the children in Year 6 at Butler Primary School will be going to in September. Twelve children will be going to Ash High.

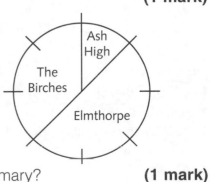

a. How many children are in Year 6 at Butler Primary?   **(1 mark)**

....

b. How many more children will go to Elmthorpe than The Birches? **(1 mark)**

....

Answers

NUMBERS

Test Yourself Questions
page 5

1 10 212   10 221   11 222
   12 112   12 121   12 221
2 875 431
3 303 > 103 < 301 > 130
4 1970
5 4 803 602

page 7

1 74 740, 74 700, 75 000
2 −8°C

Practice questions
page 9

1 3 063 902   (1 mark)
2 One million, two hundred and
   seven thousand, seven hundred
   and eight.   (1 mark)
3 **a.** 87 321   (1 mark) **b.** 12 387   (1 mark)
   c. 87 312   (1 mark) **d.** 12 378   (1 mark)
4 LXVIII, LXIX, LXXI, LXXII   (2 marks)
5 **a.** 349 080 (1 mark) **b.** 6500   (1 mark)
6 **a.** 212 313 < 213 231   (1 mark)
   b. 5 542 134 < 5 543 135   (1 mark)
7 **a.** 747 940 (1 mark) **b.** 747 900 (1 mark)
   c. 748 000   (1 mark)
8 10   Yes   (1 mark)
9 £4.00   (1 mark)
10 20 degrees (20°C)   (1 mark)

CALCULATIONS

Test Yourself Questions
page 11

1 60
2 55
3 =
4 Answers will vary – accept any two numbers
   that when subtracted one from the other
   have a difference of 5. Examples: 7 − 2;
   8 − 3; 9 − 4.

page 13

1 (6372)   (1332)
2 (520)   (6296)   (256)
3 180. Or any other three-digit number
   divisible by both 5 and 9.
4 41, 43, 47
5 3 and 6

page 15

1 **a.** 4212   **b.** 8308   **c.** 1342
2 £1.57

page 17

1 **a.** 274   **b.** 1234   **c.** 8.1   **d.** 98.24
2 65p

page 19

1 **a.** 175 122 **b.** 2345   **c.** 25 988
2 £11.25

page 21

1 **a.** 122   **b.** 29   **c.** £45.50
2. six glasses

Practice Questions
page 23

1 **a.** $(3 \times 6) + 2 < 48 - 4^2$ (1 mark)
   b. $33 - 2 \times 9 = 100 \div 4 - 10$ (1 mark)
2 Accept any two numbers that have
   a product of 18.   (1 mark)
   Examples: 18×1; 9×2; 3×6
3 **a.** ✗   (1 mark)   **b.** ✔   (1 mark)
   c. ✗   (1 mark)   **d.** ✗   (1 mark)
4 1, 2, 3 and 6
                 (1 mark: all correct for 1 mark)
5 97   (1 mark)
6 **a.** 184.27 (1 mark) **b.** 1878   (1 mark)
   c. 1904   (1 mark) **d.** 1208   (1 mark)
7 £16.10   (1 mark)
8 **a.** 15 packs   (1 mark)
   b. £18.75   (1 mark)

FRACTIONS

Test Yourself Questions
page 25

1 $\frac{2}{3}$

2 $\frac{1}{4} = \frac{3}{12} = \frac{6}{24} = \frac{12}{48}$

3 **a.** $\frac{2}{5}$ **b.** $\frac{1}{2}$ **c.** $\frac{2}{7}$

4 **a.** $2\frac{5}{8}$ **b.** $3\frac{2}{5}$ **c.** $4\frac{2}{9}$

page 27

1 $\frac{1}{4}$, $\frac{1}{2}$, $\frac{7}{12}$, $\frac{2}{3}$, $\frac{5}{6}$

2 $\left(\frac{7}{8}\right)$, $\frac{10}{12}$, $\frac{3}{4}$, $\frac{2}{3}$

3 **a.** $3\frac{4}{5}$ **b.** $\frac{7}{8}$ **c.** $\frac{17}{20}$

4 **a.** $\frac{5}{9}$ **b.** $\frac{1}{10}$ **c.** $\frac{3}{28}$

page 29
1 a. 170 **b.** 1,000 **c.** £2.16 **d.** 351
2 24
3 a. 18 **b.** $\frac{1}{9}$ **c.** $\frac{4}{9}$ **d.** $\frac{1}{20}$

page 31
1 0.0425 kg
2 8.08 cm, 8.081 cm, 8.1 cm, 8.81 cm, 8.9 cm,

page 33
1 0.375
2 0.35
3 0.86
4 75%, $\frac{3}{4}$
5 0.555

page 35
1 18.68
2 9.12 m
3 £2.64
4 £1.00

Practice Questions
page 37
1 a. $\frac{3}{4} = \frac{6}{8}$ **(1 mark)** **b.** $\frac{10}{12} = \frac{5}{6}$ **(1 mark)**
c. $\frac{15}{27} = \frac{5}{9}$ **(1 mark)**
2 a. $3\frac{1}{3}$ **(1 mark)** **b.** $6\frac{3}{4}$ **(1 mark)**
c. $6\frac{2}{9}$ **(1 mark)**
3 a. $\frac{3}{4}$ **(1 mark)** **b.** $\frac{2}{15}$ **(1 mark)**
c. $\frac{1}{24}$ **(1 mark)** **d.** $\frac{6}{18}$ or $\frac{1}{3}$ **(1 mark)**
4 6 children wear glasses **(1 mark)**
5 £5.80 a week **(1 mark)**
6 $\frac{3}{4}$ $\frac{40}{100}$ $\frac{3}{8}$ $\frac{3}{5}$

0.4 60% 0.375 75% **(1 mark)**
7 0.0977, 0.7, 0.7617, 0.7771, 0.78, 0.81 **(1 mark)**
8 £3463.50 **(1 mark)**
9 18 litres **(1 mark)**
10 86.95 **(1 mark)**

RATIO AND PROPORTION
Test Yourself Questions
page 39
1 $\frac{4}{32}$ or $\frac{1}{8}$
2 30 kg
3 30
4 3 or 48

page 41
1 72 m
2 £16.20
3 £185.50

page 43
1 Accept drawings of any three rectangles with length to width ratios of 2:1
2 18 m
3 750 m

page 45
1 52
2 64 g

Practice Questions
page 47
1 Four children are left-handed. **(1 mark)**
2 51 sweets are orange, 85 are cola and 68 are lime. **(1 mark: all correct for 1 mark)**
3 Any seven additional squares shaded to a total of nine shaded squares. **(1 mark)**
4 a. £3.56 **(1 mark)**
b. 558 **(1 mark)**
5 £31.20 **(1 mark)**
6 **(1 mark)**
7 7.5 km **(1 mark)**
8 207 children **(1 mark)**

ALGEBRA
Test Yourself Questions
page 49
1 a. 41.3 **b.** 500 **c.** 8 **d.** 27
2 28°

page 51
1 a. 3 **b.** 36 **c.** 7
2 a. 14 **b.** 9 **c.** 28

3 $p - 13$

page 53

1 a. 60 **b.** 0

2 This number sequence increases by four each time. 12, 16, 20, 24, 28 …
The numbers in the sequence are all multiples of four.
The last two digits of 248 are 48, which is a multiple of four.

Practice Questions
page 55

1 a. 14 **(1 mark)** **b.** 4 **(1 mark)**
  c. 0.5 **(1 mark)**
2 $a = 14°$ **(1 mark)** $b = 22°$ **(1 mark)**
3 $l = 12$ cm **(1 mark)**
4 a. 25 **(1 mark)** **b.** 5 **(1 mark)**
  c. 48 **(1 mark)**
5 a. 100 **(1 mark)** **b.** 11 **(1 mark)**
  c. 85 **(1 mark)**
6 $6l$ **(1 mark)**
7 18, 6, –6 **(3 marks: award 1 mark for each correct term)**
8 6.10, 5.95, 5.85, 5.80 **(4 marks: award 1 mark for each correct term)**

MEASUREMENT
Test Yourself Questions
page 57

1 1.472 m 37 800 g
2 340 g

page 59

1 a. 7200 **b.** 168
2 a. 17.48 **b.** 00.45
3 27 minutes

page 61

1 115 cm
2 a. 19 km **b.** 42 km **c.** 70 km

page 63

1 5 cm
2 112 cm^2
  100 cm^2
3 91.5 m

page 65

1 10 500 cm^3 **2** 5 cubic metres
3 20 m × 10 m × 2 m is one possible answer

Practice Questions
page 67

1 a. 905 cm **(1 mark)**
  b. 450 cm **(1 mark)**
2 a. 25 750 g **(1 mark)**
  b. 8067 g **(1 mark)**
3 a. 4.48 pm **(1 mark)**
  b. 12.30 am **(1 mark)**
4 a. 394 **(1 mark)**
  b. 285 **(1 mark)**
5 12 hrs 35 mins **(1 mark)**
6 a. 120° – 125° **(1 mark)**
  b. 55° – 60° **(1 mark)**
  c. 90° – 94° **(1 mark)**
  d. 26° – 30° **(1 mark)**
7 5250 cm^3 **(1 mark)**

GEOMETRY
Test Yourself Questions
page 69

1 An octagon
2 Because all the angles are not equal
3 Two 45° angles
4 7 faces, 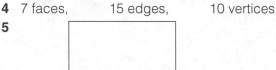 15 edges, 10 vertices
5

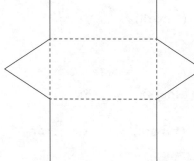

page 71

1 12.5 cm
2 450°
3 Because an obtuse angle must be more than 90° but the total of the three angles in a triangle is only 180°

page 73

1 A shape moved to a new position on a grid.
2 The distance you travel vertically along the y axis.

Practice Questions

page 75

1 Because two angles must be equal in an isosceles triangle. **(1 mark)**

2 **a.** 241°   **(1 mark)**   **b.** 129°   **(1 mark)**
   c. 12°   **(1 mark)**

3 B (5,14)   **(1 mark)**   D (–3, –4)   **(1 mark)**

4 **a.** A (–1, 4)   B (1, 4)   C (1, 3)
   D (0, 3)   E (–1, 2)   **(1 mark)**

STATISTICS

Test Yourself Questions

page 77

1 $\frac{3}{4}$

2 25%

page 79

1 **a.** 200   **b.** 400   **c.** 115–125

2 **a.** £60   **b.** £12–18   **c.** £70–80

Practice Questions

page 81

1 **a.** 540 children took part in the trial. ☑   **(1 mark)**
   b. One-quarter preferred 'Pops'. ☑   **(1 mark)**
   c. One-fifth preferred 'Hoops'. ☒   **(1 mark)**
   d. 10 percent preferred 'Bix'. ☒   **(1 mark)**

2 35   **(1 mark)**

3 3°C   **(1 mark)**

4 21 s   **(1 mark)**

SATs PRACTICE QUESTIONS

pages 82–87

1 811   **(1 mark)**

2 474   **(1 mark)**

3 82732 **(2 marks: award 1 mark for evidence of using the formal method of long multiplication which contains no more than one arithmetical error, 1 mark for correct answer)**

4 316 **(2 marks: award 1 mark for evidence of using the formal method of long division which contains no more than one arithmetical error, 1 mark for correct answer)**

5 15.9495   **(1 mark)**

6 59   **(1 mark)**

7 6   **(1 mark)**

8 $5\frac{13}{20}$ **(1 mark)**

9 $1\boxed{\frac{3}{4}} = \boxed{\frac{7}{4}}$ **(1 mark: all 4 correct for 1 mark)**

10 **a.** Section A = 24 m^2 **(1 mark)**
   b. Section B = $\frac{2}{7}$ (accept $\frac{4}{14}$)   **(1 mark)**

11 Accept, for example 6 and 1   **(1 mark: 1 mark for any correct pair of numbers)**

12 $a = 6$, $b = 12$ and $c = 8$ **(2 marks: 2 marks for all 3 correct; 1 mark for any 2 correct)**

13 900 g

   (2 marks: 2 marks for the correct answer, 1 mark for a method that would have led to the correct answer but for a computational error)

14 No   **(2 marks: 2 marks for No and a detailed explanation that includes the discounted prices of the phone at both Smartech, £123.25 and Fastfone, £128; 1 mark for No and a less detailed explanation that only includes one of the discounted prices)**

15 $x = 10$ cm   **(1 mark)**

16 **a.** $y + 3$ **(1 mark)**
   b. $5x - 6$ **(1 mark)**

17 £1.00   **(1 mark)**

18 45 cm^2 **(2 marks: 2 marks for the correct answer, 1 mark for a method that would have led to the correct answer but for a computational error)**

19 133°   (1 mark)

20 282°   (1 mark)

21 30 bottles   (2 marks: 2 marks for the correct answer, 1 mark for a method that would have led to the correct answer but for a computational error)

22

(1 mark: 1 mark for drawing the rectangle in the position indicated)

23 a. 96 children in Year 6   (1 mark)

b. 12 more children   (1 mark)

Acute – Any angle less than 90°

Addition – Joining several numbers together to find their total.

Adjacent – Corners or sides that are next to each other are adjacent.

Algebra – Maths where numbers or values are represented by letters or symbols.

Analogue – A clock with a circular face, usually marked with the numerals 1–12 and an hour and a minute hand.

Angle – The amount of turn between two straight lines that are joined at a point.

Approximately – An answer or equation that is not completely accurate but close enough to be useful. The symbol ≈ may be used to show this.

Area – The size that a surface takes up measured in 'square' **units of measurement**, for example square metres (m^2).

Capacity – The amount of liquid that a container can hold.

Common denominator – When working with fractions with different denominators, convert them to equivalent fractions with the same or common denominator. This number should be a multiple of both denominators.

Common difference – The amount that a linear number sequence increases or decreases by each time.

Continuous data – Data that has any value within a certain range, for example the temperature throughout the day.

Conversion graph – A line graph that shows the relationship between two different units of measurement.

Coordinates – Pairs of numbers that show the exact position of a point on a grid. Normally within brackets and separated by a comma.

Cube – To find the cube of a number you multiply it by itself twice. For example, 4 cubed is 64 because $4 \times 4 \times 4 = 64$. You can show that a number is cubed with a symbol, for example $5^3 = 125$.

Data – A collection of information which might be numbers, facts or measurements. Data is often organised into tables and displayed as charts or graphs to make it easier to understand.

Decimal fraction – Any fraction where the denominator is a power of 10, for example 10, 100 or 1000. Writing them with a decimal point instead of a denominator makes it easier to complete operations. Often just called decimals.

Decimal places – Decides how accurate a decimal answer is. For example a decimal rounded to one decimal place will be rounded to the nearest tenth. $3.78 \rightarrow 3.8$

Decimal point – Dot used to separate the decimal fraction from the whole part of a number.

Decreasing – Making an amount smaller.

Diagonal – A straight line that joins non-adjacent corners of a polygon.

Digit – The individual figures that numbers are made from.

Digital – A clock that shows the hour followed by the number of minutes past the hour, usually separated by a colon.

Digital sum – To find the digital sum of a number keep on adding the digits together until you get to a single digit number. For example the digital sum of 909 is 9 so you know that it is a multiple of 9. ($9 + 0 + 9 = 18$, $1 + 8 = 9$)

Division – The **inverse** of multiplication. Either think of **sharing** an amount equally (e.g. 25 sweets shared between 5 friends equals 5 sweets each) or **grouping** objects (e.g. how many half-dozen egg boxes are needed to hold 36 eggs? 6 groups of 6 equal 36).

Divisor – The amount that you are dividing by. It might be a whole number, a fraction or a decimal.

Equation – An equation uses an equals sign to separate two expressions with the same value, for example $2x = 10$ or $5 \times 3 = 10 + 5$.

Equivalent fractions – Different fractions that represent the same amount.

Estimating – Making a rough or approximate calculation to help you solve a problem.

Expression – Numbers, symbols and operation signs ($\times$, $\div$, $+$ and $-$) grouped together to show the value of something, for example $2 + 3$ or $7y + 3$.

Factor – A whole number that divides exactly into another whole number. For example, both 6 and 8 are factors of 48 because they divide into 48 without leaving a remainder.

FDP – Fraction, decimal and percentage. Three different ways of showing the same part of a quantity, total or size.

Formula – Formulae are rules that show the relationship between different **variables** in maths and science. They are usually written as **equations**.

Fraction – Any part of a number, part or whole. For example, $\frac{3}{4}$ means 3 out of 4 equal parts. The top number is the **numerator** and the bottom number is the **denominator**.

Fractions of an amount – If you divide a quantity, total or size into equal parts then these are fractions of that amount. For example a quarter of a metre is 25 cm. $\frac{1}{4}$ of 100 cm = 25 cm.

Imperial measures – Units of measurement that used to be common in the UK. Some are still used today.

Improper fractions – Any fraction where the **numerator** is bigger than the **denominator**. They are "top-heavy" fractions, for example $\frac{10}{8}$.

Increasing – Making an amount larger.

Integer – Also called whole numbers, integers can be positive or negative but not fractions or decimal numbers.

Inverse – The inverse or opposite operation can be used to check your answer. So you could check a subtraction answer by doing an addition or a division answer by doing a multiplication.

Isosceles – A triangle with two equal sides and two equal angles.

Linear number sequence – A set of numbers that increases or decreases by the same amount each time.

Mass – The amount of matter an object consists of. Your mass would be the same on Earth or in space.

Mean – Also called the arithmetic **average**. Add up all the values and divide by the number of values to find the mean.

Metric measures – A decimal system of measurement that uses multiples of 10.

Mixed numbers – Numbers that are a mix of integer and fraction, for example $4\frac{3}{5}$.

Multiple – If a number divides by another without leaving a remainder then it's a multiple of that number. For example 48 is a multiple of both 6 and 8 because 48 ÷ 6 = 8.

Multiplying – A short way to add the same number together many times, you might hear this called "lots of". You will need to know the multiplication tables.

Negative numbers – Numbers less than zero.

Non-unit fractions – Any fraction with a numerator greater than one.

Obtuse – Any angle between 90° and 180°

Operation – Grown-ups will know these as sums. They could be addition, subtraction, multiplication or division. Operations might also be things like squaring a number.

Parallel – Parallel lines always stay the same distance apart and never meet.

Partition – Breaking up a number into its separate parts, for example hundreds, tens and ones, to help you complete operations like multiplication.

Percentage – A percentage is a fraction out of 100 and is usually shown using the % symbol.

Perimeter – The distance around the outside of a shape. The perimeter of a circle is called the **circumference**.

Perpendicular – Perpendicular lines are at a right angle (90°) to each other.

Pie chart – A special chart that shows the relative sizes of data as sectors of a circle.

Place value – The position or place of each digit decides what value it has in the number.

Polygon – Any 2D shape with straight sides.

Polyhedron – A 3D shape with flat faces.

Prime number – A whole number that has exactly two factors, one and itself. For example, 7 only has factors 1 and 7. 1 doesn't qualify because it only has one factor!

Proportion – A part of an amount compared to the whole. For example the proportion of white cars is one in every five. You can write this as a fraction $\frac{1}{5}$.

Quadrant – The four areas that are created when you divide a grid with an *x* and a *y* axis.

Ratio – Compares different parts of the whole amount to each other. For example the ratio of red to white cars is three to four. You can write this as a ratio, 3:4.

Reasoning – Explaining and justifying your answer, for example by showing how you know that something is correct.

Recurring decimal – Decimals that have a repeating digit or a repeating pattern of digits. You might round them to a number of decimal places or use a symbol to show that they recur. For example $\frac{1}{3}$ can be shown as 0.3̇

Reduce – Simplify a fraction to get the lowest **numerator** and **denominator** possible.

Reflection – A shape that is reflected is flipped across a mirror line without changing its size.

Reflex – Any angle between 180° and 360°

Regular – A polygon that has all sides and all angles equal.

Remainder – What's left over when the number you are dividing is not a multiple of the divisor. You can write it as a whole number (**integer**), fraction or decimal. In problems you usually have to round your remainder either up or down.

Roman numerals – A number system using seven letters to represent number values.

Rounding – Changing a number to a more convenient value, for example the nearest ten, hundred or thousand.

Scale factor – A ratio that expresses the amount of enlargement or a ratio between two sets of measurements.

Scale – If you scale something you reduce or enlarge all of its dimensions. The scale of a map or drawing refers to the ratio between the measurements on the model or drawing and the size of the actual object or distance. A scale can also be a set of marks on a measuring instrument.

Sequence – An ordered set of numbers, shapes or objects arranged according to a rule.

Similar – Shapes that are similar are the same shape as each other but not the same size.

Simplify – Divide both numbers in a fraction, ratio or proportion by the same number to make them easier to understand.

Square – To find the square of a whole number, you simply multiply it by itself. For example 4 × 4 = 16. You can show that a number is squared with a symbol, e.g. $9^2 = 81$.

Straight angle – An angle that is exactly 180°.

Subtracting – Taking one number away from another. You might hear it called 'the difference between', 'minus' or simply 'taking-away'.

Term – One of the numbers in a sequence.

Translation – To move or "slide" a shape to a new position on a grid without changing its size or appearance.

Unit fractions – Any fraction with a **numerator** of 1.

Units of measurement – Most mathematics in real life involves money or measures. When giving an answer to a problem, remember to include the correct units of measurement, for example euros (€) or square metres (m^2).

Variable – A value in an equation that is represented by a symbol or letter.

Volume – The volume is the amount of space taken up by a three-dimensional (3D) object. It is measured in cubic units, for example cubic centimetres (cm^3)

Weight – The **mass** of an object multiplied by gravity.

Index